Cryptocur~~r~~

The Comprehensive Manual For Harnessing The
Technological Revolution. Acquire The Knowledge Of
Engaging In Metaverse Investments, Nft And Earning
Through Crypto Trading And Virtual Land Acquisition

ANEAS THALLER

Alternative Cryptocurrencies To Bitcoin

Bitcoin has emerged as the prevailing standard in the realm of cryptocurrencies, an occurrence that has notably sparked an increasingly expansive community of enthusiasts and subsequent derivatives. Bitcoin has not only served as a pioneer, stimulating the emergence of numerous cryptocurrencies founded on a decentralized peer-to-peer network, but it has also established itself as the prevailing benchmark for cryptocurrencies, fostering an ever-expanding community of devotees and offshoots.

- In a comprehensive sense, a cryptocurrency refers to a form of currency that exists on a distributed and decentralized ledger, taking the form of tokens or "coins."

- Furthermore, given Bitcoin's inception more than ten years ago, the realm of cryptocurrencies has experienced remarkable expansion, potentially leading to the emergence of another groundbreaking digital token in the near future.

- Bitcoin remains the front-runner among cryptocurrencies in terms of market capitalization, user base, and overall performance.

- Ethereum and various other digital currencies are being utilized to construct decentralized financial frameworks for individuals lacking access to traditional financial products.

- Certain alternative cryptocurrencies are being upheld due to their provision of innovative functionalities that surpass Bitcoin. These functionalities include the ability to process a higher number of transactions per second and the implementation of diverse consensus algorithms, such as proof-of-stake.

What Are Cryptocurrencies?

Prior to delving into any of these alternative options to Bitcoin, it would be prudent to pause and establish clear definitions for terms such as cryptocurrency and altcoin. In its most expansive connotation, a cryptocurrency embodies a virtual or digital medium of exchange presented as tokens or "coins." Although certain cryptocurrencies have materialized in the physical realm via credit cards or other endeavors, the overwhelming majority of cryptocurrencies persist as wholly intangible entities.

The expression "crypto" pertains to the intricate cryptographic techniques facilitating the generation and handling of digital currencies alongside their transactions within decentralized systems. The predominant inclination towards decentralization aligns closely with the fundamental "crypto" nature of these currencies; cryptocurrencies are typically constructed as software by developer teams who incorporate mechanisms for issuance (commonly, though not exclusively, via a procedure referred to as "mining") and other regulatory measures.

Cryptocurrencies are predominantly designed to be impervious to government manipulation and regulation, although this inherent aspect of the market has faced criticism with its growing adoption. Alternative cryptocurrencies, colloquially referred to as "altcoins," and occasionally derogatorily referred to as "shitcoins," are digital currencies that have been designed based on the model of Bitcoin with the intention of presenting themselves as improved or revised iterations of Bitcoin. While it is true that certain alternative currencies may possess distinct characteristics not found in Bitcoin, none of these altcoins have thus far achieved the same level of security offered by Bitcoin's network.

In addition to Bitcoin, we will now examine several prevalent digital currencies. However, it is important to state a caveat before proceeding: it is impossible for a list of this nature to be entirely comprehensive. One possible reason for this phenomenon can be attributed to the fact that, as of January 2021, there exists a staggering number of more than 4,000 cryptocurrencies in active circulation. While it is the case that certain cryptocurrencies lack substantial support or trading volume, there are also some which are backed by dedicated groups of supporters and investors.

Furthermore, it should be noted that the landscape of cryptocurrencies is in a state of perpetual transformation, with the potential for the emergence of significant new digital currencies in the near future. Whilst Bitcoin is commonly acknowledged as the earliest form of cryptocurrency, analysts employ diverse approaches when assessing tokens beyond BTC. Financial analysts, as an illustration, often assign significant importance to the relative market capitalization rankings of various coins. This has been duly considered, however, there exist alternative justifications for the inclusion of a digital token in the aforementioned list.

1. Ethereum (ETH)

Ethereum, being the initial substitute for Bitcoin in our inventory, is an autonomously operating software platform enabling the development and execution of Smart Contracts and Decentralized Applications (DApps) without necessitating the involvement of external entities, thus eliminating the risks associated with downtime, theft, control, or intervention by third parties. The objective of Ethereum is to establish an inclusive range of decentralized financial offerings that are accessible to individuals around the globe, without any discrimination based on nationality, race, or religion, and at no cost. This attribute amplifies the repercussions experienced by individuals residing in specific nations. Individuals lacking access to government infrastructure and official identification have the opportunity to acquire banking facilities, loans, insurance, and a range of other financial services.

Ethereum applications are motivated by ether, the platform-specific cryptographic token of the Ethereum network. Ethereum utilizes ether as a means of facilitating transactions and enabling movement on its blockchain network. It is predominantly sought after by software developers looking to construct and operate applications on the platform, as well as investors seeking to acquire alternative digital currencies using ether. Ether, which made its debut in 2015, holds the position of the second-most significant digital currency in terms of market capitalization, trailing only Bitcoin. Despite this, Ether has yet to bridge the considerable gap that separates it from the leading cryptocurrency. As of January 2021, the market capitalization of Ethereum amounts to approximately 19 percent of that of Bitcoin.

In 2014, Ethereum initiated a pre-sale for ether, eliciting an extensive and profound reaction, subsequently marking the commencement of the era of initial coin offerings (ICOs). According to the organization, Ethereum can be utilized to "formally document, distribute authority, safeguard, and facilitate transactions involving a wide range of assets." After the occurrence of the 2016 DAO attack, there was a divergence within the Ethereum blockchain, resulting in the creation of two separate branches: Ethereum (ETH) and Ethereum Classic (ETC). In January 2021, the market capitalization of Ethereum (ETH) amounted to $138.3 billion, while each token held a value of $1,218.59.

In 2021, Ethereum aims to transition its consensus algorithm from proof-of-work to proof-of-stake. This modification would facilitate a reduction in energy consumption within Ethereum's network, alongside an enhancement in transaction processing velocity. Proof-of-stake enables users to securely deposit their ether on the network for validation purposes. This procedure contributes to enhancing network security while also facilitating transaction processing. Individuals engaging in this activity are remunerated with ether, reflecting an equivalent value commensurate with the interest earned on a savings account. This presents a viable alternative to Bitcoin's proof-of-work mechanism, wherein miners are remunerated with additional Bitcoin for facilitating transaction processing.

2. Litecoin (LTC)

Litecoin, having made its debut in 2011, is considered among the early entrants in the cryptocurrency arena, emulating the path laid out by Bitcoin and earning the moniker of "silver" to Bitcoin's "gold." Its creator, Charlie Lee, is an alumnus of MIT and a former engineer at Google. Litecoin operates on a decentralized global payment network, built upon open-source technology. It is not subject to control or oversight by any central authority. The network employs a consensus mechanism known as "scrypt" proof of work, which enables the decoding of transactions using standard consumer-grade CPUs. While there are similarities between Litecoin and Bitcoin, such as their underlying principles, Litecoin distinguishes itself with a more expedient rate of block generation and quicker transaction confirmation time. A growing multitude of retailers, alongside developers, show their endorsement for Litecoin. In January 2021, the global cryptocurrency market recognized Litecoin as the sixth-largest digital currency, as it possessed a market capitalization of \$10.1 billion and an individual token value of \$153.88.

3. Cardano (ADA)

Cardano is a cryptocurrency based on the "Ouroboros proof-of-stake" consensus algorithm, created by a team of engineers, mathematicians, and cryptography experts who have employed a research-oriented approach in its development. Charles Hoskinson, a distinguished individual among Ethereum's initial cohort of founders, played a key role as a co-founder in the establishment of the project. Following some divergences in regard to the trajectory of Ethereum, he made the decision to part ways and subsequently played a pivotal role in the establishment of Cardano.

Cardano's blockchain underwent rigorous testing and meticulous scrutiny by the Cardano team, as substantiated by thorough peer-reviewed studies. The researchers affiliated with the project have authored and disseminated more than 90 scholarly publications that delve into diverse aspects of blockchain technology. The foundation of Cardano lies in the research conducted by its team.

Cardano emerges as a notable choice among its counterparts in the proof-of-stake realm and other prominent cryptocurrencies owing to this meticulous approach. Cardano has garnered the moniker of the "Ethereum killer" due to the formidable prowess of its blockchain technology. Alternatively, Cardano is at an early developmental stage. Despite achieving success in implementing a proof-of-stake consensus paradigm ahead of Ethereum, there is still a significant journey ahead for the platform to fully embrace decentralized financial applications.

Cardano aims to establish itself as the global financial operating system, harnessing decentralized financial products just like Ethereum. Moreover, it provides solutions for chain interoperability, prevention of voter fraud, and scrutiny of legal contract tracking, amongst other endeavors. As of January 2021, Cardano possesses a market capitalization totalling $9.8 billion, while the valuation of a single ADA stands at $0.31.

4. Polkadot (DOT)

Polkadot is an unparalleled proof-of-stake digital currency that endeavors to facilitate the seamless interoperability of blockchain technology. Its established protocol facilitates the interoperability of both permissioned and permissionless blockchains and oracles, enabling seamless collaboration among diverse systems within a unified framework.

The relay chain of Polkadot represents its primary element, facilitating the seamless exchange of data and operations across various networks. Additionally, it facilitates the implementation of "parachains," which are parallel blockchains equipped with their own native tokens designed for specific and distinct purposes.

Instead of exclusively focusing on constructing decentralized applications on Polkadot, developers have the opportunity to construct their own blockchain while concurrently deriving advantages from the security and safeguard offered by Polkadot's chain. Developers have the capability to construct fresh blockchains utilizing Ethereum; however, they are required to incorporate their own security protocols. This implementation process exposes nascent and lesser-scale projects to potential breaches, as the size of a blockchain directly correlates with its level of security. The term "shared security" is what Polkadot employs to describe this concept.

Gavin Wood, an additional founding member of the Ethereum project, harboring differing perspectives regarding the project's trajectory, was instrumental in the creation of Polkadot. The market capitalization of Polkadot stands at $11.2 billion, as per the data of

January 2021, with the value of one DOT estimated at $12.54.

5. Bitcoin Cash (BCH)

Considering its status as an early and widely embraced hard fork of the original Bitcoin, Bitcoin Cash (BCH) occupies a noteworthy position within the historical landscape of altcoins. A division arises within the cryptocurrency ecosystem due to conflicting perspectives and discussions among developers and miners. Because of the decentralized existence of digital currencies, wholesale adjustments to the code underlying the token or coin in question need consensus; this process's mechanism differs by cryptocurrency.

When disparate factions are unable to reach a consensus, the digital currency undergoes a division. The initial blockchain adheres to its original protocol while the subsequent blockchain emerges as a revised iteration of the preceding cryptocurrency, incorporating modifications in its code.

Consequently, one of these ruptures led to the birth of BCH in August 2017. The discussion that ensued prior to the creation of BCH was centered on the issue of scalability, as the Bitcoin network was constrained by a block size restriction of one megabyte (MB). The block size of BCH has undergone an augmentation from one MB to eight MB, with the anticipation that the inclusion of larger blocks will facilitate the accommodation of a greater number of transactions, consequently leading to an enhanced transaction speed. In addition to this, further enhancements entail the removal of the Segregated Witness protocol, thereby impacting the allocation of block space. In January 2021, the market capitalization of BCH amounted to $8.9 billion, accompanied by a per-token valuation of $513.45.

6. Stellar (XLM)

Stellar serves as an inclusive and decentralized blockchain infrastructure, facilitating seamless connections among financial institutions in order to furnish comprehensive enterprise solutions tailored specifically for high-volume transactions. Significant financial transactions between banks and investment firms, formerly characterized by protracted durations, involvement of multiple intermediaries, and substantial expenses, can now be executed nearly instantaneously, devoid of intermediaries and with minimal or negligible costs incurred by the relevant parties.

Notwithstanding its characterization as an enterprise blockchain geared towards institutional transactions, Stellar remains an inclusive blockchain accessible to all individuals. The device enables cross-border transactions in any currency. Lumens represent the indigenous digital currency of Stellar, commonly referred to as XLM. In order for network participants to engage in transactions, possession of Lumens is a prerequisite.

Jed McCaleb, a key contributor to Ripple Labs and the innovator behind the Ripple protocol, was responsible for the inception of Stellar. He subsequently departed from Ripple and proceeded to establish the Stellar Development Foundation alongside his co-founders. As of January 2021, the market capitalization of Stellar Lumens stands at $6.1 billion, with a pricing of $0.27 per unit.

7. Chainlink

Chainlink is an automated, decentralized oracle network that establishes a seamless linkage between smart contracts, specifically those on the Ethereum blockchain, and external data sources. Blockchains are unable to securely establish connections with external applications. Smart contracts have the ability to interact with external data through the utilization of

Chainlink's decentralized oracles, enabling their execution based on data that Ethereum cannot directly associate with.

An assortment of application scenarios for Chainlink's framework are explicated on the company's blog. One of the numerous cited applications is the surveillance of water sources in designated urban areas aimed at detecting instances of contamination or unlawful extraction. Sensors can be implemented to oversee corporate utilization, water tables, and regional water levels. This data has the potential to be monitored and accessed through a Chainlink oracle, enabling its seamless integration into a smart contract. Based on the data received from the oracle, the smart contract has the capability to impose penalties, deliver flood notifications to municipalities, or generate invoices for companies that excessively consume water within a given urban area.

Sergey Nazarov and Steve Ellis engaged in a collaborative effort for the development of Chainlink. As of January 2021, the market capitalization of Chainlink amounts to $8.6 billion, with each individual LINK token valued at $21.53.

8. Binance Coin (BNB)

Binance Coin serves as a functional digital currency within the Binance Exchange, facilitating the payment of transactional fees. Those who utilize the token for payment during the transaction will vend at a discounted price. The blockchain of Binance Coin also serves as the underpinning for Binance's decentralized exchange platform. Changpeng Zhao is the mastermind behind the inception of the Binance exchange, which has gained immense recognition on a global scale due to its substantial trading volumes.

The initial issuance of Binance Coin took place in the form of an ERC-20 token deployed on the Ethereum blockchain. It was ultimately granted its primary network. The network employs a consensus model based on proof of stake. As of January 2021, Binance's market capitalization stands at $6.8 billion, while the value of a single BNB coin is $44.26.

9. Tether (USDT)

Tether emerged as an early and prominent player among stablecoin cryptocurrencies, a subset of digital currencies that strive to mitigate volatility by linking their market valuation to a specific currency or external benchmark. Tether and other stablecoins strive to mitigate market volatility in order to attract consumers who may have concerns regarding digital currencies, including prominent ones such as Bitcoin that have experienced recurring periods of significant instability. The value of Tether is inherently tied to the value of the United States dollar. The framework facilitates expedited and convenient conversions from alternative digital currencies to US dollars, surpassing the traditional conversion process to fiat currency.

Tether, a company that was founded in 2014, presents itself as a "platform empowered by blockchain technology aiming to facilitate the widespread adoption of fiat currencies in the digital realm." Through this cryptocurrency, users are able to engage in transactions using traditional currencies on a decentralized network, effectively circumventing the volatility and uncertainties typically associated with digital currencies. Tether held the position of being the third most prominent digital currency in terms of market capitalization during the month of January 2021. It possessed a cumulative market capitalization of $24.4 billion, with each individual token being valued at $1.00.

10. Monero (XMR)

Monero is a cryptocurrency that prioritizes security, anonymity, and non-traceability. This decentralized digital currency, which operates under an open-source protocol, was initially launched in April 2014. Its emergence swiftly resonated with connoisseurs of cryptography. The development of this digital currency is entirely financed through charitable contributions and supported by the collective. Monero was developed with significant focus on decentralization and scalability, and it employs a methodology called "ring signatures" to ensure complete confidentiality.

Through this approach, a collective set of cryptographic signatures is generated, ensuring the presence of at least one genuine participant. However, as all of them seem to be valid, it becomes difficult to ascertain which one is the genuine article. Monero has acquired a dubious reputation as a result of its exceptional security measures, and it has been implicated in illicit activities on a global scale. If Monero is considered to be suitable for clandestine criminal transactions, its ability to safeguard privacy also proves advantageous for individuals opposing oppressive regimes across the globe. In January 2021, Monero's market capitalization amounted to $2.8 billion, while the value of each token stood at $158.37.

Facilitate independent verification of legislative cases. The company has stated that Sweden, Estonia, and Georgia are currently engaging in experiments pertaining to blockchain-powered land registries, potentially enabling efficient resolution or prevention of property disputes.

Blockchain Security

An adverse consequence of technological progress has manifested in the rise of unauthorized acquisition of personal data. The pursuit of digital programmers revolves around the acquisition of government data sets. Data breaches have exposed the personal information of millions of Americans, such as names, Social Security numbers, dates of birth, addresses, and driver's license numbers, as exemplified by the 2017 Equifax data breach. Booz Allen Hamilton has determined that incorporating blockchain technology enhances network security by minimizing vulnerabilities, thereby rendering data breach attempts more challenging.

The Department of National Security is currently undertaking an investigation into how blockchain can be utilized to address concerns pertaining to information security, such as the management of online identity and internet access. According to McKinsey, the technology has the capability to store encrypted versions of citizen records on the blockchain, enabling governments to provide an authenticated digital copy of these documents when necessary.

Expanding government Responsibility

In explicit utilizations, blockchain has the potential to reduce government redundancy, streamline operations, mitigate audit difficulties, enhance security, and ensure the integrity of data. One interaction that is in need of refinement is the GSA's Fastlane cycle, which is responsible for reviewing incoming proposals from vendors. Currently, Booz Allen Hamilton necessitates a period of 40 days to process incoming submissions. In any event, the General Services Administration remains confident that implementing a blockchain solution will effectively address these issues within a span of 10 days.

Lessening Government Debasement

Although blockchain technology cannot entirely prevent misconduct, the World Economic Forum (WEF) has identified five use cases to mitigate deficiencies in governmental systems.

•Public Acquisition/Government Contracting

The World Economic Forum (WEF) has indicated that public procurement is the most significant realm within government operations, holding substantial potential for corruption on a global scale. A blockchain-enabled system can operate under external supervision of transactions, offering enhanced impartiality and consistency through the implementation of automated contracts. Additionally, there would be enhanced transparency and accountability of transactions and participants. Regardless, the efficacy of its implementation may be undermined by the manner in which it is transmitted. The World Economic Forum stated that as the accessibility and usability of the blockchain platform increase, so does the vulnerability to potential misuse. Additionally, should the continuation of disconnected transactions persist beyond the scope of the blockchain stage, the potential for counterfeiting will be significantly curtailed.

•Land Title Libraries

As previously mentioned, the utilization of blockchain technology enables select countries to enhance efficiency within their land title registries. The World Economic Forum has indicated that Honduras and India have embarked upon integrating blockchain technology in order to enhance property rights and improve transparency in a system notorious for its corrupt practices. Land vaults built on the blockchain have the potential to establish a secure, decentralized, verifiably immutable, and unalterable system of records, enabling individuals to substantiate their land rights. A hindrance would arise in cases where countries lacking physical libraries would be required to construct and digitize the data before the implementation of blockchain technology could take place.

•Electronic Democratic

Legislatures are contemplating the adoption of blockchain-enabled voting platforms in light of concerns regarding the security of elections, the integrity of voter registration, the transparency of the voting process, and the level of voter participation. The data security features of blockchain technology could potentially address instances of political election manipulation and enhance the transparency of voting. According to the World Economic Forum (WEF), a limitation of blockchain technology is its vulnerability to cyber threats and various security concerns.

•Secure Corporate Asset Safes

According to a report by the World Economic Forum (WEF), clandestine networks provide avenues for illicit money laundering, exert influence over business transactions, and manipulate government initiatives. Under the implementation of blockchain technology, it is possible to establish centralized repositories that can effectively track and mitigate instances of conflicts and criminal activities. Furthermore, it has the potential to enhance transparency and visibility. However, it should be noted that there are certain limitations in place as the majority of countries do not require networks to independently maintain accurate ownership information. Likewise, a blockchain-based vault would require purchase in from government officials, legal counsellors, banks, and enormous business, which might be a weighty lift in certain areas.

•Award Payment

Considering the significant amount of funding granted to various foundations, the opaque nature of the gift process is prone to shortcomings and corruption. Implementation of blockchain technology has the potential to reduce the number of entertainers and administrators, streamline the process, and enhance the verification procedures. The World Economic Forum stated that individuals lacking a certain level of technical proficiency could potentially be disqualified from the distribution of rewards. In addition, it fails to adequately address the question of how recipients would choose to allocate and utilize the awarded funds.

What potential disruptions can Blockchain cause in enterprises?

Several prominent companies like Unilever, Walmart, Visa, among others, have implemented blockchain technology, resulting in advantages such as enhanced transparency, heightened security, and improved traceability. Considering the benefits presented by blockchain, it will significantly transform and redefine multiple domains.

Presented below are the five predominant enterprises that are likely to be adversely impacted by the rapid integration of blockchain technology:

1.Banking

2.Cyber Security

3. The Committee for Supply Chain Management

4.Healthcare

5.Government

1. Banking

Prior to Blockchain

Banking incurs additional fees, which can prove to be both expensive and cumbersome for individuals. Furthermore, the process of transferring cash overseas proves to be significantly more cumbersome due to the fluctuating exchange rate and additional hidden charges.

After Blockchain

Blockchain eliminates the need for an intermediary. Blockchain is disturbing the financial framework by giving a distributed instalment framework with the most noteworthy security and low charges.

• The utilization of blockchain technology facilitates swift and seamless cross-border payments worldwide.

•Digital currencies such as Ethereum and bitcoin negate the need for a third party to carry out transactions.

• The blockchain maintains a publicly accessible ledger of all transactions that is universally available to bitcoin users.

We should contemplate the creation of an illustrative representation of ABRA.

• Abram is a financial digital currency platform that facilitates peer-to-peer financial transactions.

•By utilizing this application, individuals who use digital currency can conveniently store, transfer, and receive their virtual funds on their electronic devices.

2. Network safety

Prior to Blockchain

Previously, cyberattacks posed a significant threat to the general public. Several organizations were developing a compelling solution to safeguard the data from unauthorized access and tampering.

After Blockchain

• The decentralized nature of blockchain ensures prompt detection of malicious attacks, as the interconnected network prohibits any alterations to the data.

- All data stored on the blockchain network undergoes verification and encryption using a cryptographic algorithm.

•Through the removal of the integrated framework, blockchain provides a transparent and secure methodology for documenting transactions (without disclosing sensitive information to any parties).

As an example, Guardtime, a product security network, provides blockchain-based products and services.

Instead of adhering to the integrated framework, the network employs blockchain technology and disseminates information to its nodes.

3. Management of the inventory network

Prior to Blockchain

Due to the lack of transparency, supply chain management often encountered difficulties such as service redundancy, inadequate interdepartmental coordination, and a lack of reliability.

After Blockchain

The implementation of blockchain technology enables the tracking and traceability of items throughout the entire inventory network, ensuring transparency and accountability.

Blockchain enables the ability for the office to verify and evaluate transactions conducted by multiple supply chain partners connected to the inventory management system.

• The blockchain system documents the complete transaction details (including historical information, timestamp, and date) of an item within a decentralized distributed ledger.

• Each transaction is documented and stored in a block.

• The utilization of blockchain technology allows for universal verification of the authenticity or current condition of a conveyed item.

Allow Us To Explore A Visual Representation Of The Pacific Fish Project.

In this context, blockchain supply chain management offers a systematic verification process to track seafood. The process facilitates the prevention of illegal fishing.

4. Medical services

Prior to Blockchain

In the context of the healthcare services framework, patients have the ability to align themselves with various clinics and promptly access their medical records. In addition to the delay, there is a significant risk of information degradation due to the storage of data in a physical memory system.

After Blockchain

- Blockchain eradicates a centralized authority, thus facilitating immediate access to data.

- In this arrangement, every block is interconnected with an additional block and allocated throughout the PC hub. This poses a substantial challenge for a programmer to compromise the integrity of the data.

One example of this is Joined Medical Care, an American medical network that has enhanced its coverage, confidentiality, and interoperability of clinical records through the implementation of Blockchain technology.

5. Government

Prior to Blockchain

The act of tampering with votes is a criminal offense that occurs within the majority of conventional democratic systems. Similarly, constituents who wish to exercise their right to vote are required to patiently wait in a queue and submit their ballots to a nearby authority, which can be an extremely time-consuming process.

After Blockchain

• Citizens are allowed to vote without the requirement of disclosing their identity in public.

• The authorities meticulously count the votes, ensuring that each identification can be attributed to a single vote.

• Once the vote is entered into the public record, it becomes permanently irremovable.

Consider a visual representation depicting Mi Vote.

• Mi Vote is a decentralized blockchain platform that shares resemblances with a digital voting booth.

• By employing Mi Vote, individuals are able to cast their votes using their mobile devices, ensuring that voting records are securely stored in the blockchain.

Moving forward, let us delve into the fundamentals of Blockchain.

Generating an NFT entails the act of producing a digital asset. It encompasses a diverse range of creative expressions, including but not limited to digital art, photography, videography, animation, and musical compositions, among other possibilities. You might be familiar with anecdotes of a plain black backdrop fetching substantial sums, among numerous comparable instances. This is the reason why this section is associated with the Reality Check of NFTs section.

If you possess expertise in the field, you should have no difficulty in generating various forms of digital creative materials. Alternatively, if you do not possess professional expertise, there are numerous methods available to generate NFTs.

If you, as a skilled professional, possess the ability to craft exceptionally remarkable and one-of-a-kind artwork, it truly doesn't get any better than that. I would like to emphasize the importance of promptly taking appropriate measures.

The focus lies less on the work itself, instead emphasizing the importance of hype, marketing strategies, and current trends. There is no need for you to devise a completely novel approach; rather, observe the effective strategies employed by others and endeavor to develop a similar concept.

A highly effective method for identifying trends is by monitoring not only platforms such as Twitter and other social media networks but also the NFT marketplace.

Canva can also be utilized. It is imperative that you refrain from employing the work of others, as doing so may potentially expose you to legal complications. You have the ability to create designs that are fundamental yet aligned with either the potential emerging trends or the current prevailing ones.

An alternative approach would be to enlist the services of a freelance designer. This represents unequivocally the most straightforward approach to acquire expertly crafted NFTs without expending any effort. It is advisable to establish a clear understanding with the freelancer from the outset, indicating your intention to engage their services specifically for the purpose of creating an NFT. Doing so will help prevent potential conflicts down the line, particularly in the event that the NFT gains significant popularity. A few independent contractors are in fact engaging in this practice. Fiverr is the optimal location for the acquisition of services of this nature. Clicking on this link will lead you directly to the page dedicated to NFT freelancers.

Please bear in mind the fundamental principles of human psychology when designing the NFT. Consumers make purchase decisions influenced by their emotional state, and in a thriving market such as the current one, emotions are particularly heightened. We are discussing emotional experiences such as the Fear Of Missing Out (FOMO).

How NFTs Work

In the preceding chapter, I have established the groundwork to facilitate your comprehension of Non-Fungible Tokens (NFTs) by elucidating their non-interchangeability, tracing their historical origins, and illustrating their intricate association with cryptocurrencies. Gaining comprehension of the operational mechanisms of NFTs will facilitate a deeper understanding of the underlying concept they represent.

Blockchain-Based

Prior to the advent and widespread acceptance of NFTs, non-fungible digital assets have been in existence since the early stages of the internet. These non-fungible digital assets encompass various in-game items, including in-game currencies, domain names, event tickets, and user handles on social media platforms such as Twitter. Nevertheless, these non-fungible digital assets exhibited a range of differences in terms of standardization, liquidity, interoperability, and tradability.

Consequently, although we possess numerous non-fungible digital assets, we have never truly possessed any of them in the genuine guise of ownership. As an illustration, in the case of purchasing a skin on Fortnite, you acquire ownership of the corresponding in-game item within the game. It is not permissible for individuals to make the decision to extract the skin from their Fortnite game and subsequently engage in its sale within a secondary marketplace such as eBay. Likewise, it is imperative to note that the skin acquired for Fortnite cannot be utilized within alternative gaming platforms such as PlayerUnknown's Battlegrounds (PUBG). Consequently, the possession of non-fungible digital assets is entirely contingent on the context. In other words, your ownership of specific digital assets is limited to the platform that offers them.

Nevertheless, the predicament of ownership was effectively resolved by the advent of Non-Fungible Tokens (NFTs), given that each NFT is anchored to a specific blockchain. Blockchains serve as a means of harmonizing digital assets, bestowing users with the rights of ownership and management authorization. With the utilization of blockchains, individuals have the ability to exercise full ownership over a digital asset reliant on blockchain technology, thereby granting them the liberty to possess and transfer said asset for an indefinite duration. Additionally, blockchain-based digital assets encompass a variety of distinctive attributes that reshape the interactions between users and developers with respect to said assets.

Blockchain-based non-fungible tokens possess inherent characteristics that distinguish them from conventional digital assets. Some of the characteristics present in this include the subsequent:

Standardization

As previously stated, there is a variation in standardization among traditional digital assets, which depends on both the specific type of digital asset and the platform upon which they are issued. It

48

should be noted that there is currently no uniform representation of traditional digital assets within the digital realm. As an illustration, the manner in which a game depicts an in-game item will contrast with the manner in which an event ticket is depicted in an event ticketing system. Nevertheless, through the application of blockchain technology, creators have the capacity to establish universally applicable standards that are both reusable and inheritable, thereby facilitating the representation of Non-Fungible Tokens. These standards encompass fundamental elements such as straightforward entry restriction, ownership privileges, and transfer privileges for any blockchain-powered NFT.

If there is a requirement to incorporate specific supplementary criteria into specific NFTs, for instance, guidelines pertaining to the presentation of a particular NFT, it is feasible to seamlessly integrate these standards with the pre-existing ones. Implementing an additional framework of guidelines will subsequently equip creators with a fresh set of foundational principles known as stateful rudimentary fundamentals.

Interoperability

In contrast to conventional digital assets, the transferability of Non-Fungible Tokens across various ecosystems is facilitated by the standardized framework of blockchain-based NFTs. Consequently, once a developer establishes a new Non-Fungible Token endeavor, the project promptly becomes visible within virtual realms, accessible through various wallet providers, and open to trading on diverse market platforms. The attainment of interoperability stems from the establishment of blockchain standards, which furnish an unclouded, uniform, dependable, and regulated Application Programming Interface (API). This API facilitates the seamless retrieval and insertion of data.

Tradability

In essence, the compatibility of blockchain-backed NFTs facilitates the seamless and convenient exchange of these NFTs across diverse online market platforms. In addition, the interoperability aspect of blockchain-enabled non-fungible tokens facilitates unrestricted trading within open marketplaces. This implies that, in contrast to conventional digital assets, individuals utilizing blockchain-based digital assets have the capability to transfer possessions from their original settings to alternate marketplaces to facilitate their sale. This affords the users of blockchain-based digital assets the opportunity to leverage sophisticated trading functionalities, including auctioning akin to eBay, packaging different items together, engaging in bidding activities, and conducting sales in diverse currencies such as stablecoins and currency specific to the application.

Liquidity

It is to be expected that there will be an increase in liquidity as a result of the immediate tradability of non-fungible tokens (NFTs). Hence, as long as NFTs continue to rely on blockchains, developers will not encounter any liquidity issues. Moreover, with the proliferation of NFT marketplaces, NFTs gain enhanced visibility and access to a large pool of potential buyers and sellers.

The concepts of unchangeability and verifiable limitation

Due to the blockchain nature of NFTs, creators have the ability to employ smart contracts, enabling them to limit the quantity of NFTs and establish immutable attributes for their NFTs post-issuance. For example, a developer has the ability to programmatically ensure the production of a distinct quantity of a scarce digital asset, just as they can programmatically ensure the production of an unlimited quantity of a widespread digital asset.

Furthermore, it is possible for a developer to enforce particular immutable properties on specific digital assets through the utilization of on-chain encoding. This is particularly advantageous for digital art assets that significantly depend on the verifiable rarity of an authentic artwork.

Programmability

In the realm of digital assets, NFTs and traditional counterparts bear a common attribute, namely their inherent programmability. Certain functions can readily be incorporated into non-fungible tokens prior to their release. As an illustration, CryptoKitties incorporated a reproductive mechanism within their tokenized digital felines. This implies that the fusion of two felines can result in the reproduction of a completely novel variety of cat.

Currently, NFT developers are inclined towards incorporating intricate mechanics into their NFTs, encompassing elements such as random generation, forging, crafting, redeeming, and so forth. The NFT universe offers a vast array of programming opportunities that are virtually limitless.

Ethereum Token Standards

In the Ethereum network, tokens have the capacity to embody various forms, encompassing but not limited to lottery tickets, the abilities possessed by a character within a game, and even financial assets such as shares of a company. Hence, the establishment of a robust ecosystem on Ethereum, or any comparable blockchain, necessitates the seamless interaction between each token. As an illustration, let us consider a scenario in which two tokens were generated, each possessing distinct configurations of intelligent agreements. In order for both tokens to establish interoperability, it will be necessary for their developers to diligently examine each contract and devise a comprehensive plan for their harmonious functioning. Accordingly, this endeavor may pose challenges to scalability. Now, let us envision a scenario where there exist 1,000 distinct tokens, each endowed with 1,000 unique smart contracts. The process of determining the precise qualifications and specifications required for the seamless interoperability of all 1,000 tokens necessitates an extensive amount of intricate computations, which is a time-intensive endeavor and falls short of an optimal situation. This is the rationale behind the development of token standards, which aim to establish standardized guidelines for governing the fundamental structure of tokens on Ethereum's blockchain. These regulations are referred to as "ERC," an acronym for "Ethereum Request for Comment." Correspondingly, the numerical suffix appended to "ERC," like ERC-20, denotes distinct token standards.

Standards for Non-Fungible Tokens beyond the Ethereum ecosystem.

Regarding the development and facilitation of Non-Fungible Tokens, it is currently noticeable that Ethereum's network stands as the most advanced and user-friendly platform accessible for such purposes. Nevertheless, alternative networks employ standards distinct from Ethereum when generating an NFT. Let us examine some of those alternate networks.

dGoods

The dGoods standard is a publicly available and complimentary protocol that facilitates ownership and enhanced tradability of digital goods and assets utilizing blockchain technology. The platform offers cross-chain functionalities, facilitating seamless interoperability between two distinct blockchains. This interoperability feature facilitates communication between distinct blockchains, as these blockchains adhere to a standardized framework. The current functionality of the platform enables the seamless integration of two distinct blockchains, namely Microsoft Azure and EOS, in order to facilitate cross-chain operations. There are ongoing endeavors to expand this capability to encompass additional independent blockchains in the foreseeable future. Nevertheless, at present, NFTs generated utilizing the dGoods protocol will possess the capability to engage with both EOS and Microsoft Azure's blockchain networks.

COSMOS

Cosmos represents a distributed network comprising autonomous parallel blockchains, thereby denoting the platform as an ecosystem encompassing numerous interconnected blockchains. The platform functions as a network of interconnected blockchains, intended to facilitate decentralized communication amongst themselves. Therefore, similar to dGoods, the blockchains within the Cosmos platform possess the ability to seamlessly communicate and exchange data with one another.

This platform achieves inter-platform compatibility through the utilization of a collection of open-source tools including Tendermint, The Cosmos SDK, and IBC. These aforementioned open-source tools enable individuals to create bespoke, fortified, adaptable, and compatible blockchain applications.

The development team of the platform is presently working on the creation of a standalone NFT module, which has been integrated into the Cosmos SDK. Consequently, NFTs generated utilizing the Cosmos Standard will possess the capacity to seamlessly operate across various blockchains with no limitations.

FLOW

Flow is an emerging blockchain platform designed to provide the underlying infrastructure for next-generation applications, games, and various forms of digital assets. The development team responsible for the creation of the CryptoKitties game has pioneered a novel programming paradigm referred to as Cadence, which operates on the blockchain technology known as Flow. This software application facilitates the conversion of non-fungible tokens (NFTs) into resources that can be securely stored by the users within their respective accounts. The Cadence programming language upholds significant ownership regulations which are rigorously implemented by the platform. The regulations governing the programming framework guarantee that all non-fungible tokens produced using the Cadence standard inherently possess a solitary proprietor and are safeguarded against unintended or deliberate duplication or loss. The crux of these regulations lies in their provision of safeguards, ensuring that owners can have peace of mind, knowing that their NFTs are securely upheld as digital assets with tangible worth.

Chapter Two: The prevailing cryptocurrencies in circulation

In the forthcoming chapter, we shall examine the prevailing/prominent cryptocurrencies.

Bitcoin

Bitcoin was the inaugural example of a digital currency and has subsequently become the predominant and prevalent cryptocurrency in current times. This particular currency was formulated by an individual named Satoshi Nakamoto and was subsequently introduced to the general public through online platforms in the year 2009. The cryptocurrency is commonly acknowledged as the "currency of the people" owing to the remarkable progress it has achieved since its inception on the Internet. The payment network derives its power from its users, functioning as a decentralized peer-to-peer payment network, as intended. Transactions in Bitcoin do not involve any higher authorities or intermediaries. Bitcoin is commonly regarded by users as a form of currency optimized for online usage as it is both mined and transacted primarily on the Internet.

The Bitcoin network lacks a designated controller, much like how no individual holds exclusive ownership of the underlying technology of email. Bitcoin is governed by individuals who are utilizing the digital currency on an international scale. Software developers may endeavor to enhance the software, but they lack the capacity to enact a substantial alteration to its underlying protocol. Individuals are afforded the option to select a particular iteration of Bitcoin that aligns with their preferences, provided it adheres to the requisite protocols associated with the original software. Due to this fact, both users and developers have a profound inclination to safeguard this agreement.

From the standpoint of a user, Bitcoin can be regarded as a software application that enables individuals to engage in transactions involving their digital wallets. The sole distinction lies in the fact that, as opposed to utilizing conventional currency for transactions, users are instead engaging in transactions through the use of cryptocurrency. A significant level of expertise is not necessary for this task. This is the typical operational mechanism of cryptocurrency for the majority of users.

There exists a prevailing belief among individuals that Bitcoin payments pose a significant level of difficulty, however, this concept is considerably removed from reality. Bitcoin transactions offer greater convenience compared to using credit or debit cards for making purchases. It also presents a significantly more cost-effective option. Bitcoin payments can be facilitated using either a personal computer or a conventional smartphone, as long as one possesses the requisite wallet application. To effectuate a payment, kindly input the designated payee's address, indicate the precise amount owing, and transmit the transaction accordingly. Wallets have the capability to receive recipient addresses through the utilization of QR codes or by utilizing NFC technology, a technology that is commonly found on the majority of smartphones.

Ethereum

Blockchain technology is not exclusively linked to Bitcoin. It would be incorrect for one to assume that Bitcoin is the sole form of cryptocurrency in existence. Bitcoin is, in fact, one of numerous applications that leverage Blockchain technology in contemporary times.

Ethereum represents an additional software platform that operates on the principles of Blockchain technology. It provides developers with the ability to construct and implement applications that possess the inherent characteristic of being decentralized.

There exists a prevalent misconception wherein individuals perceive Ethereum and Bitcoin as indistinguishable, however, this notion is fallacious. Ethereum and Bitcoin possess the common characteristic of being public, decentralized Blockchain networks. However, it should be emphasized that their primary distinction resides in their intended purpose and capacity. Bitcoin offers a specific implementation of Blockchain technology, which operates on a decentralized digital currency framework. This system facilitates digital transactions involving Bitcoin to be conducted online. The Bitcoin blockchain serves the purpose of maintaining a comprehensive record of all Bitcoin transactions conducted within the platform. Regarding the Ethereum blockchain, its primary function pertains to executing the program code of decentralized applications developed on the platform.

In the Bitcoin network, mining operations are being conducted by miners in order to acquire Bitcoin. The cryptographic token associated with Ethereum is commonly referred to as Ether. This is the objective that miners strive to achieve. Ether is the essential factor responsible for the proper functioning and maintenance of the network. Programmers employ tokens as a means of remunerating for various services or fees rendered within the Ethereum network. Individuals also have the option to utilize the token as a negotiable form of virtual currency.

For Ethereum to function effectively, it is imperative that the platform engages a minimum number of several thousand individuals who execute the software on their computers, thereby enabling the network to operate smoothly. Each computer, referred to as a node, within the network operates an entity known as the Ethereum Virtual Machine (EVM). The EVM can be characterized as a system that understands and carries out the software authored in an Ethereum-specific programming language, functioning akin to an operating system.

Ripple

As previously stated, the foundation of cryptocurrency technology lies in the principle of decentralization. However, ripple takes a more traditional approach. By leveraging blockchain technology, it presents an essential enhancement to the SWIFT banking concept, thereby offering a highly sought-after improvement.

Presently, the transmission of conventional currencies through the SWIFT system necessitates the involvement of numerous intermediaries and entails a considerable time frame. The procedure exhibits lower levels of security and a higher degree of risk compared to the offerings presented by Ripple. However, ripple offers expedited and more cost-effective transactions which are initiated through the utilization of a singular currency, XRP. At present, the ripple team has established partnerships with more than 100 banks globally, which encompass esteemed financial institutions such as ATB Financial, CIBC, UBS, Standard Chartered, among others.

Monero

Monero enables users to conduct transactions in a manner that ensures privacy by preventing the disclosure of public transaction records accessible through the blockchain. By default, all transactions conducted with Monero ensure complete privacy. If one places utmost importance on privacy, Monero fulfills all the requirements. The currency has been intentionally designed to possess complete anonymity and to be practically untraceable. This extends to their development team, which, unlike other cryptocurrencies, lacks a publicly known CEO or prominent figure.

Furthermore, Monero utilizes "ring signatures," an advanced cryptographic technique aimed at guaranteeing the anonymity of transactions. This feature enables the users to receive funds anonymously, ensuring that the recipient's address cannot be traced back to the sender. This could be regarded as either beneficial or detrimental, depending on one's perspective towards the concept of anonymity. The ring signatures further obscure not only the identities of the buyer and seller, but also the monetary value involved in the transaction. In contrast to Dash, Monero has maintained an open-source approach since its inception, which allows unrestricted access to the software code for the sake of complete transparency.

The currency's underlying veil of anonymity has rendered it a preferred choice among dark web users. Prior to its closure, the Darknet marketplace known as AlphaBay had implemented Monero alongside Bitcoin in order to facilitate its transactional operations. The platform facilitated the exchange of various illicit items such as illegal drugs, firearms, and stolen credit cards. In addition to its anonymous nature, Monero has garnered favor among individuals engaging in ransomware activities.

It is yet to be determined whether Monero will expand its applications to include concealing an individual's actual wealth, or if it will persist as the preferred cryptocurrency for illicit sectors, thereby inhibiting its widespread adoption compared to other cryptocurrencies. This prevailing uncertainty could be strategically leveraged by speculators aiming to capitalize on the vast potential for widespread adoption.

Litecoin

Litecoin, the initial alternative cryptocurrency, has exemplified modest yet consistent development within a digital currency landscape driven by exaggerated enthusiasm and significant periods of fluctuation. As a result of this, numerous analysts have labeled it as the "coin with low-risk potential." Introduced in 2011 with the objective of serving as "the silver counterpart to Bitcoin's gold" and addressing the limitations faced by Bitcoin at that time, Litecoin possesses a coin limit that is four times higher than that of Bitcoin, totaling 84 million coins. This distinct feature renders Litecoin a deflationary currency as well.

The period required for block creation amounts to 2.5 minutes, which constitutes a mere one-fourth of

Bitcoin's 10-minute interval. Prior to the ascendance of Ethereum in 2017, Litecoin enjoyed the notable distinction of being the second most significant cryptocurrency in terms of market capitalization.

The expeditious generation of blocks in Litecoin provides a significant edge over Bitcoin, as it enables Litecoin to efficiently process a larger number of transactions. This indicates that merchants have the capability to utilize rapid payment transfers without incurring any transaction fees. Contrarily, Bitcoin would require four times the duration to facilitate an equivalent transaction, all the while incurring greater expenses. Litecoin is also distinguished by its exceptionally active team of developers within the cryptocurrency realm. Thanks to this committed group, the coin consistently undergoes state-of-the-art enhancements; for instance, it was notably the first coin to adopt the innovative Segregated Witness (SegWit) technology. Furthermore, this attribute bestows upon the coin the benefit of possessing the second most impervious blockchain subsequent to the one belonging to Bitcoin.

An additional benefit for prospective investors is the level of acceptance on prominent exchanges. A vast majority of the largest cryptocurrency exchanges have extended their support for purchasing Litecoin with fiat currency. A notable development in this regard occurred in March 2017, when Coinbase, a prominent player in the industry, embraced Litecoin, thereby offering a valuable opportunity for investors from the United States and the European Union. With regard to market dynamics, it is generally observed that Bitcoin and Litecoin exhibit a parallel trend in relation to fluctuations in their respective currency valuations. Numerous investors opt for Litecoin as an supplementary choice to Bitcoin, with the aim of enhancing portfolio diversification.

For those interesting in mining, Litecoin's algorithm is far simpler which makes the mining costs and barriers to entry lower. Litecoin operates using the Scrypt algorithm, while Bitcoin operates using the SHA-256 algorithm. From a practical standpoint, the primary implication of this is a reduction in mining expenses, as Scrypt places less strain on Graphics Processing Units (GPUs). In the current year of 2017, undertaking Bitcoin mining has become unfeasible for individuals lacking expertise or conducting operations from their households. Conversely, engagement in Litecoin mining can yield financial gains, even after taking into account expenses related to electricity consumption within developed nations.

Litecoin has faced criticism from its detractors, who argue that the coin lacks innovation and is merely a replication of Bitcoin. Furthermore, in 2015, the coin fell prey to a pump-and-dump scheme orchestrated by Chinese investors, who acquired and subsequently dumped 22% of the total available coins.

Factom

Similar to Ethereum, Factom aims to extend the applications of blockchain technology beyond solely serving as a medium for digital currency. While Ethereum operates on a foundation of dual authentication and guarantying the inviolability of contracts, Factom pledges to achieve a similar level of security for extensive data sets through the establishment of an unalterable record system. This would enable enterprises and governmental entities to present a verifiable history of data without any modification or loss. Some examples of the practical uses encompassed by this phenomenon are within the realms of legal proceedings, corporate financial management, the organization and maintenance of medical records, and even the facilitation of electoral processes. Envision, if you will, a realm where the act of manipulating electoral outcomes or the occurrence of deceitful financial practices akin to Enron's downfall were utterly unattainable.

Similar to other initiatives that employ blockchain technology, Factom remains immutable due to its decentralized nature, where no singular individual exercises control over the network. The network is communally owned by a significant number of users, operating autonomously from one another. While data under the control of a single individual is susceptible to malicious activities, unauthorized access, accidental mistakes, and tampering, such risks are non-existent when it comes to data owned collectively by a network of individuals.

In relation to investment matters, similar to how Ether corresponds to Ethereum, Factoids represent the designated "currency" within the Factom system. The increased utilization of Factom in generating applications corresponds to a commensurate increase in the value of Factoids. Factom has successfully entered into an agreement with the esteemed consulting firm, iSoftStone, to offer cutting-edge blockchain-powered administrative software projects for municipalities in the People's Republic of China. The agreement encompasses provisions for the provision of auditing and verification services.

According to the CEO of Factom, Peter Kirby, it is believed that this technology will assist developers in establishing a novel category of accountable and unalterable business systems. This can be found in various industries such as insurance, financial services, medical records, or real estate - in any sector where meticulous record keeping is imperative."

Similar to other blockchain technologies, typical inquiries surrounding Factom pertain to its scalability and broader adoption within the technological realm. The other main drawback to Factom investing is whether the team can run the system at a consistent profit going forward - or whether the technology will lead to a race to the bottom in terms of price.

Golem

Golem represents a form of cryptographic currency, ingrained within the Ethereum blockchain network. Termed by certain analysts as the "Airbnb of computing," the primary focal point of the coin's worth lies within the software applications it enables.

The creators of the Golem Project designate it as a "high-performance computing system" that possesses the capability to establish connections with additional computers to serve diverse objectives. These encompass scientific inquiry, rigorous data examination, and the extraction of digital currency. As an illustration, in the event that your computer possesses unutilized computational capabilities, it is feasible to lease such capacities to another individual in need by means of the Golem network, thereby drawing a parallel with the Airbnb concept. The individual requiring additional computational capacity possesses the capability to obtain processing power equivalent to that of a supercomputer, at a significantly lower expense compared to the actual ownership of such processing power.

In theory, it is undeniably obvious that users have the potential to generate income from their underutilized computational resources. However, what is yet to be determined is the tangible implementation of this technology. The diminished prominence of marketing efforts from the Golem team has seemingly exerted a detrimental effect on the value of the coins in recent times. The absence of the capability to purchase GNT with fiat currency, including USD, also presents a limitation for the broader consumer base.

It is important to acknowledge that the technology is presently in its nascent stages of development, and as of August 2017, the team is actively seeking alpha testers for the project. The Golem Project has a significant likelihood of diminishing into insignificance. Conversely, there exists considerable potential for substantial future growth considering that the coin's price remains below $0.30.

The durability and resilience of blockchain technology:

Blockchain technology possesses inherent resilience, much akin to the internet. Due to the storage of identical information blocks throughout its network, the blockchain is rendered incapable of:

Be subject to the influence of any singular entity.
Does not possess a singular point of failure.

Bitcoin was first created and unveiled in the year 2008. Ever since, the Bitcoin blockchain has been functioning without any significant disruption. Thus far, any issues pertaining to Bitcoin have arisen exclusively from instances of hacking or mismanagement. Put differently, these difficulties arise as a consequence of malevolent intent and human fallibility, rather than imperfections in the foundational principles.

The internet has demonstrated remarkable resilience over a span of nearly three decades. The aforementioned record signifies promising prospects for the ongoing advancement of blockchain technology.

Transparent and incorruptible:

The blockchain network exists in a state of consensus, wherein it periodically verifies its own integrity every ten minutes. A self-regulating ecosystem of digital value, the network verifies and reconciles all transactions occurring at ten-minute intervals. Each set of these transactions is commonly referred to as a "block". Consequently, two significant characteristics derive from this:

By its very nature, transparency data is inherently public as it is integrated into the entirety of the network.
The incorruptibility of the blockchain lies in the fact that any attempt to modify a single unit of information within it would necessitate a substantial computational effort capable of overriding the entire network.

From a theoretical standpoint, this could potentially be feasible. In practical application, it is improbable to occur. Gaining authority over the system with the objective of seizing Bitcoins, for instance, would equally result in the depreciation of their worth.

2.4 The Blockchain: A Paradigm Shift for Cryptocurrency and the Internet

The blockchain empowers individuals on the internet to generate value and verify the integrity of digital data. What will be the outcome of the implementation of novel cryptocurrency business applications?

Smart contracts:

Distributed ledgers facilitate the encoding of uncomplicated agreements that will be executed upon the fulfillment of predefined criteria. Ethereum, a decentralized cryptocurrency, is an open-source blockchain initiative developed with the explicit purpose of achieving this objective. However, during its nascent phase, Ethereum possesses the capability to harness the efficacy of blockchains on a profoundly transformative level.

Given the present state of technological advancement, smart contracts have the capability to be programmed in order to execute basic operations. For example, a derivative has the potential to be disbursed upon the fulfillment of specific criteria of a financial instrument, employing blockchain technology and Bitcoin to automate the payout process.

The sharing economy:

With the prosperity of companies such as Uber and Airbnb, it is evident that the sharing economy has unquestionably demonstrated its accomplishments.

Presently, nevertheless, individuals desiring to request the services of a ride-sharing platform are compelled to depend on a mediator such as Uber. Through the facilitation of peer-to-peer transactions, the blockchain affords the opportunity for direct engagement between individuals, consequently engendering a genuinely decentralized sharing economy.

An initial instance, Open Bazaar utilizes the blockchain technology to establish a decentralized online marketplace akin to a peer-to-peer version of eBay. Install the application onto your computing device, and you will be able to engage in transactions with Open Bazaar vendors without incurring any transaction fees. The absence of rules guiding the protocol implies that personal reputation will hold an even greater significance in business interactions compared to its existing importance on eBay.

Crowd Funding:

Crowdfunding platforms such as Kickstarter and Gofundme are laying the groundwork for the nascent peer-to-peer economy. The widespread use of these platforms indicates a strong desire among individuals to actively participate in the process of product development. Blockchains elevate this interest to a higher magnitude, aspiring to establish crowd-funded venture capital funds.

In the year 2016, an exemplary undertaking, known as the Ethereum-based DAO (Decentralized Autonomous Organization), managed to amass a staggering sum of $200 million USD within a span of slightly over two months. The individuals acquired "DAO tokens," granting them the ability to partake in voting for investments in smart contract venture capital (the extent of their voting influence was determined by the amount of DAO they possessed). The subsequent breach of project funds demonstrated that the project was initiated without sufficient scrutiny, leading to catastrophic outcomes. In any case, the experiment conducted by the DAO indicates that the blockchain holds promise in facilitating "a transformative model of economic collaboration."

Governance:

Through the implementation of distributed database technology, elections and other forms of polling could achieve complete transparency by ensuring that the results are readily accessible to the general public in a fully transparent manner. Ethereum-based smart contracts facilitate the automation of the process.

The application known as Boardroom facilitates the execution of organizational decision-making processes on the blockchain. In practical application, the result entails a complete display of transparency and verifiability in corporate governance while handling digital assets, equity, or information.

Supply chain auditing:

Customers are displaying an escalating desire to ascertain the validity of the ethical assertions made by companies regarding their merchandise. Distributed ledgers offer a convenient means to authenticate the veracity of the origins associated with our purchases. The introduction of blockchain-based timestamping allows for the verification of a product's date and location, thereby enhancing transparency. This is particularly relevant in the case of ethical diamonds, where the said information is associated with a unique product number.

Provenance, a company headquartered in the United Kingdom, provides supply chain auditing services for various consumer products. Through the utilization of the Ethereum blockchain, a Provenance pilot initiative guarantees that the fish being sold in Sushi establishments in Japan has been procured in a sustainable manner from its suppliers in Indonesia.

File storage:

Implementing a decentralized approach to file storage on the internet yields evident advantages. The dissemination of data across the network helps safeguard files from unauthorized access or accidental loss.

Inter Planetary File System (IPFS) makes it easy to conceptualize how a distributed web might operate. In a manner analogous to the data transmission mechanism of bit torrent, IPFS abolishes the necessity of centralized client-server associations, thereby effectively replacing the existing web structure. A hypothetical scenario where websites are entirely decentralized has the capability to enhance the efficiency of file transmission and streaming durations. This improvement not only offers convenience, but also provides additional benefits. It is an essential enhancement to the existing overburdened content-delivery systems on the internet.

Prediction markets:

The utilization of crowdsourcing to obtain predictions on the probability of events has been substantiated to possess a considerable level of precision. The process of obtaining an average of opinions mitigates the influence of unexamined biases that compromise rational judgment. Prediction markets that remunerate participants based on the results of events are presently operational. Blockchains are an exemplar of collective intelligence technology that undoubtedly will discover additional utility in the forthcoming years.

However, while still in its Beta phase, Augur, the prediction market application, facilitates the issuance of shares based on the anticipated outcome of real-world events. The participants have the opportunity to generate income by making an accurate investment in the correct anticipation. The greater the number of shares acquired in the accurate result, the greater the payout will be. By making a modest financial contribution (amounting to less than one dollar), individuals are afforded the opportunity to pose inquiries, establish markets reliant on projected outcomes, and receive fifty percent of the total transaction fees generated by the market.

"Safeguarding of intellectual property:

It is a widely acknowledged fact that digital information possesses the remarkable ability to be endlessly replicated and effortlessly shared, primarily facilitated through the vast infrastructure of the internet. This has presented internet users across the globe with a valuable resource of cost-free content. Nevertheless, the copyright holders have experienced a lack of fortune, relinquishing their authority over their intellectual property and enduring financial repercussions as a result. Smart contract technology has the capacity to safeguard intellectual property rights and enable automated transactions for digital creative works on the internet, mitigating the potential hazards associated with unauthorized duplication and redistribution.

Mycelia utilizes the blockchain technology to establish a decentralized music distribution system among peers. Established by the British singer-songwriter Imogen Heap, Mycelia offers musicians the opportunity to directly sell their songs to audiences, as well as grant licenses for samples to producers and distribute royalties to songwriters and musicians. These various functionalities are facilitated through the implementation of intelligent contracts. The potential of blockchains to enable fractional cryptocurrency payments (micropayments) indicates a high probability of success for this particular application of the technology.

The Benefits And Drawbacks Of Cryptocurrencies

Cryptocurrencies facilitate the seamless transfer of payments between two entities in a transaction without the need for an intermediary financial institution such as a bank or credit card company. These transfers are facilitated through the utilization of public and private keys, as a measure to ensure enhanced security. In contemporary cryptocurrency systems, it is standard for each user's wallet or account address to possess public accessibility. In addition, it possesses a private key that will be utilized for the purpose of signing transactions. Fund transfers are accompanied by low processing fees, thereby enabling consumers to evade the exorbitant charges associated with wire transfers commonly imposed by banks and financial institutions.

The underlying technology utilized by Bitcoin, known as blockchain, serves as a crucial element in the attractiveness and operational effectiveness of the currency. This technology facilitates the storage of a comprehensive online ledger, documenting all Bitcoin transactions. Notably, the blockchain structure is robust against potential security breaches by malicious entities and can be seamlessly replicated across all computer systems running Bitcoin software. Prior to generation, each starting block must undergo verification by the ledgers held by individual users within the marketplace. This renders the fabrication of transaction histories unattainable. Numerous enthusiasts regard this blockchain technology as a commonly employed protocol for facilitating online voting and crowdfunding activities. Prominent financial institutions also anticipate the potential for cryptocurrencies to reduce transaction fees through the enhancement of payment transactions and processes, leading to heightened efficiency.

One drawback associated with these cryptocurrencies pertains to their virtual nature, resulting in the absence of a centralized repository. The equilibrium of these digital cryptocurrencies may become inaccessible and be erased in the event of a computer malfunction, unless a backup of these assets is preserved or their private keys are not inadvertently misplaced. Furthermore, there is an absence of a central authority that can access funds or information when employing these virtual currencies.

The inherent semi-anonymous characteristics of cryptocurrencies render them highly conducive to a wide array of nefarious activities, including but not limited to money laundering and the circumvention of tax obligations. This facilitates greater recognition of cryptocurrencies while ensuring anonymity, with certain cryptocurrencies offering even greater levels of privacy compared to others. Bitcoin, as an illustration, is an unsuitable option for engaging in illicit business activities and online transactions. Based on the meticulous forensic examination of these transactions, law enforcement officials have successfully apprehended and detained these perpetrators. In contemporary times, an increasing number of privacy-centered cryptocurrencies such as Dash and Zcash are being employed with heightened difficulty in their traceability.

The valuation of cryptocurrencies is determined by the interplay of market demand and supply dynamics in the economic sphere. The exchange rate has the potential to experience significant fluctuations. Further investigations are currently underway to ascertain the primary driver of price fluctuations in these cryptocurrencies. Bitcoin has also undergone significant fluctuations and increases in value. The value of Bitcoin experienced a significant decline, reaching as low as $19,000 in December 2017, and subsequently fluctuating around $7,000 in the subsequent months. Economists perceive this to be a transitory occurrence within a perceptive speculative trend. The issue at hand pertains to the precedence of currency units, given their lack of tangible backing in material assets. In addition, it has been acknowledged by certain individuals that the production costs of these cryptocurrencies exhibit a direct correlation with their market value, necessitating a progressively greater energy expenditure.

The blockchain networks of these cryptocurrencies are indeed protected but remain susceptible to the potential risk of unauthorized access through hacking. Over the course of the past decade, Bitcoin has witnessed multiple instances where online exchanges were compromised and resulted in incidents of theft. However, numerous aficionados of numismatics regard these cryptocurrencies as a potential avenue for preserving their monetary worth. Additionally, it can be expedited and possesses greater portability and adaptability compared to rigid metals. Additionally, it operates beyond the scope of central banking institutions and governmental authorities.

Blogs and Emails

This approach is highly effective. In the event that a customer has made a prior purchase and expressed satisfaction with your product or services, it is highly likely that they will make a repeat purchase. Utilizing resources such as establishing personal blogs or similar platforms can prove highly effective in generating sales and increasing traffic to your store. There are numerous means by which one can obtain unfettered traffic without financial obligation. Today, our focus will be restricted to discussing the aforementioned primary aspects, namely blog creation and email list acquisition. Now, it is important to note that there is a drawback to this approach, as it may require a significant amount of time to attract traffic to your blog and build your email list. Therefore, if your objective is to achieve expedited outcomes, I would advise against employing this particular method.

The utilization of blogs and email lists as a means of promoting products and services has been a long-standing practice. Many prosperous drop-shipping enterprises rely exclusively on this approach to promote their products and services. Thus, it functions effectively and with impressive results. However, please be mindful that immediate success is not to be expected, as it necessitates a certain amount of time. Now, taking that into consideration, I would like to present the three key factors that necessitate your attention prior to commencing the advertising campaign using this particular approach.

Establish an online platform for publishing content, such as a blog.

- Drive traffic to the blog
- Obtain email subscribers - Gather email recipients - Acquire email subscribers - Garner email contacts - Secure email subscribers
Please refrain from sending them unsolicited mass emails.

The initial step that must be undertaken is to establish a blog. To effectively commence the collection of emails, it is imperative that you initiate the creation of a blog. So, the process of collecting emails is relatively straightforward. After establishing your blog, I would like you to initiate the practice of publishing content centered around the particular niche or subject matter that aligns with your store or product. As an illustration, should your online store or product pertain to fishing, consider composing a blog post focused on topics such as 'mastering the technique of ice fishing' and the like. Ensure that the content of your blog is replete with valuable information. Individuals would be disinclined to subscribe to a blog in the event that it fails to exude a sense of exhilaration or furnish them with exceptional insights and strategies pertaining to the particular subject matter.

Now that you have established a blog and composed your initial post, it is crucial to commence the promotion of your blog within targeted circles. This can be accomplished without incurring any cost. To obtain the desired information, simply access the Google search engine and query for blogs that have been posted within a 24-hour period. Please proceed to the comment section of their blog and kindly encourage each reader to visit your link. This strategy has proven to be highly effective in generating organic traffic.

Once your website begins to generate traffic, it is now appropriate to commence the process of gathering email addresses. To ensure the receipt of emails, provide an incentive. Therefore, in the event that your blog and online store are in the realm of fitness, it would be advantageous to offer individuals a complimentary workout plan upon submission of their email address. It is widely acknowledged that the allure of free goods and services is highly appealing, thus it is crucial to ensure that such offerings are made available to your audience. This method is likely to assist you in building an extensive email database. I want to emphasize that I have personally utilized this technique to successfully accumulate approximately 10,000 email addresses, thus I strongly recommend its implementation.

Once you have acquired a substantial number of emails, you may commence the promotion of your products. However, it is imperative to bear in mind that spamming is strictly discouraged. Consistently bombarding individuals with sales-oriented emails on a daily basis tends to elicit negative responses; thus, it is crucial to exercise prudence and ensure an appropriate time interval between each communication. In an optimal scenario, this is the suggested approach for initiating communication with your prospective client via email. During the initial four days, it is recommended to dispatch an informative email such as "guidance on fishing" or "a guide to physical exercise." The content should ideally be relevant to your website's theme. Following this, on the fourth day, you may proceed with promoting your product. This method typically proves effective for me, and I am confident it would yield positive results for you as well.

Given the array of resources at your disposal, you should now possess the capacity to establish your own drop-shipping store. Bear in mind that achieving your desired outcome requires a significant investment of both time and effort. However, once financial inflows are established, the endeavor will become highly automated, subsequently facilitating the realization of your long-held aspirations.

Bitcoin Trading Process

The core essence of Bitcoin revolves around the act of trading. Due to its non-recognition as a formally acknowledged currency, individuals have the ability to engage in Bitcoin transactions and subsequently exchange their Bitcoin holdings for various commodities. There exists a multitude of methods through which one can engage in Bitcoin trading, along with various activities that can be undertaken. Bitcoin is highly suitable for facilitating transactions ranging from conventional currency and residential properties, to even mundane items such as groceries. In order to ensure optimal financial outcomes while utilizing Bitcoin for trading purposes, it is imperative to adhere to proper trading practices and mitigate any potential monetary losses arising from transactions conducted with the Bitcoin assets under your ownership.

For Services

Online-based services constitute the predominant proportion of services viable for trade with Bitcoin. Certain individuals who utilize Bitcoin may opt to engage in transactions involving:

Website creation

Content marketing

Site enhancement

Computer optimization

Given that Bitcoin is a digital form of currency and facilitates online transactions, its utility is particularly pronounced within the realm of online commerce. Previously, individuals engaged in these activities and exchanged goods had to make payments through the utilization of a credit card (which involves potential hazards) or by employing a payment service such as Paypal (which can be excessively convoluted).

The inception of Bitcoin greatly simplifies the process of individuals engaging in online transactions and remunerating for digital services. It is a resource that can be of advantage to all individuals. In the event that you do not possess a website, have no requirement for content marketing, or have no inclination to establish a website in the future, it is feasible to utilize Bitcoin as a medium of exchange for procuring a service that will significantly enhance the performance of your computer beyond its previous capabilities.

By availing yourself of each of these services, you will enhance your overall computer or technology experience. If you desire to enhance the overall experience, opting to exchange it for Bitcoin would streamline the process of payment for said services. Bitcoin facilitates seamless payments and enables effective communication with individuals offering their services.

For Goods

There is a plethora of goods available for online purchase. A significant portion of these products can be located within the online marketplace, and a considerable number of prominent online retailers have recently adopted the acceptance of Bitcoin as a viable payment method. You have the capability to utilize your Bitcoin wallet at the prevalent merchants, thereby facilitating a streamlined and fortified digital shopping venture. In order to utilize your Bitcoin when transacting with an e-commerce establishment:

Discover the desired items and proceed to accumulate all desired purchases within the shopping cart or shopping bag on the platform of the respective retailer.

Please proceed to the shopping cart or bag and carefully review the items that you intend to purchase.

Please utilize the designated checkout button.

Locate the establishment that accepts Bitcoin as a form of payment.

Please provide your personal information to facilitate the shipment of your articles.

Please locate the designated area and input your Bitcoin wallet identification to facilitate payment for the merchandise.

Confirm the purchase

Your Bitcoin wallet will be updated automatically with the purchase information, and the corresponding amount will be deducted from it. You are not required to wait for a statement or any other form of clearance, as the process is instantaneous.

Traditional Trades

Bitcoin is an advantageous asset to possess for engaging in trade-related investments. These types of investments encompass assets such as equities, fixed-income securities, and even diversified investment vehicles like mutual funds. One may execute a similar action using their Bitcoin by procuring them solely for the purpose of investment.

If one were to consider alternative investment options or even retain the funds in the form of conventional currency held in a savings account, it would require a significant amount of time for the accumulated capital to generate a substantial return on the initial investment. The yields of even the most competitive high-interest savings accounts are considerably lower than the returns generated from your investments in Bitcoin.

Another advantageous feature of engaging in investment-oriented trading activity with Bitcoin is the avoidance of the obligation to allocate it to a particular account for the purpose of enhancing its overall worth. Simply allow it to remain in your wallet where the remainder of your Bitcoin is stored. This will enable it to appreciate in value as the overall value of Bitcoin continues to expand. Within a year's time frame, there exists the potential for you to recover as much as 25% (or potentially even more) of your initial investment.

When You Purchase

When purchasing Bitcoin, it is imperative to ensure that you do so at an advantageous timing. The optimal time to purchase Bitcoin is during the weekends and in the early morning prior to the market's opening. This is an imperative task to undertake in order to ensure that you secure the most favorable price. Monitor the fluctuations in the Bitcoin prices over a span of several days to identify the point at which it reaches its minimum value.

By purchasing Bitcoin at its minimum value within a period of five days, you will have the opportunity to generate a return on your investment automatically, thereby ensuring that you are effectively gaining profit from your Bitcoin holdings. It would be advisable to consider purchasing it solely when it reaches its lowest possible price point. Considering the individuals who were early adopters of Bitcoin, it is probable that they invested a nominal amount, possibly a few dollars, which has since grown exponentially to a valuation in the millions.

Purchasing at the opportune moment will greatly influence your capacity to garner profits through Bitcoin.

When conducting the sale

Contrarily, when selling Bitcoin, it is crucial to exercise caution and attentiveness in order to secure the most advantageous price. Additionally, it is imperative to consider the associated selling fee when attempting to sell it on platforms such as Coin Base, as failure to execute the transaction at an opportune moment may result in a financial loss. By capitalizing on its peak value, you will have the opportunity to secure the necessary profits in order to acquire additional Bitcoin and subsequently replicate this cycle.

When opting to sell your Bitcoin at its peak value, it is important to bear in mind the likelihood of subsequent depreciation, which warrants due consideration during the selling process. Once the sale has been completed, it is advisable to closely observe the price fluctuations for a few days. Allocate the generated profits from the sale towards the acquisition of additional quantities of the comparatively inexpensive Bitcoin. This method presents the most straightforward and efficient approach to maximize financial gains through Bitcoin. There exists minimal or negligible waiting duration during the purchase and selling of Bitcoin, enabling swift profit generation.

Exchanging Bitcoin

Although it is common knowledge that Bitcoin can be exchanged for goods and services, it is also noteworthy that there exist alternative avenues on the Internet through which Bitcoin can be traded. If you are utilizing Bitcoin, you have the option to engage in exchanges for other Bitcoin, diverse forms of digital currency, or even for various commodities in your possession. For instance, should you possess an exceptionally distinct or scarce item, you may effectively employ it as a means of exchanging it for Bitcoin.

Given that Bitcoin lacks official recognition as a currency and is not subject to regulatory oversight, it possesses the versatility to be employed in a wide array of transactions and applications. This implies that you have the option to request three Bitcoin from someone in exchange for a book that they desire. It is important to bear in mind that there are no established protocols or regulations for trading or selling commodities using Bitcoin.

Hence, caution should be exercised when pursuing Bitcoin acquisition. Determining the appropriate remuneration or acceptable form of compensation can pose challenges and intricacies.

When engaging in the utilization of Bitcoin, it is of utmost importance to exercise caution due to its lack of regulation. While it is possible to acquire substantial sums for items of relatively lesser value, there is also a risk of falling victim to fraudulent practices associated with Bitcoin. It is imperative to consistently possess an understanding of the inherent worth of commodities being transacted, including an awareness of the prevailing value of Bitcoin.

What Is The Monetary Worth Of Digital Currency?

Bitcoins possess inherent worth due to their widespread acceptance for transactions.

When asserting that the currency is backed by gold, we are alluding to the existence of a facility wherein one can convert currency into gold. Initially, Bitcoin was devoid of any inherent value. However, as it gained wider acceptance, individuals commenced trading tangible commodities in exchange for this digital currency, leveraging its capacity for instantaneous transactions.

Essentially, one could argue that bitcoin is underpinned by the valuation assigned to goods by sellers, specifically the pledged exchange of goods for a particular currency value.

Bitcoin, along with the currencies of pound, euro, and dollar, possesses value solely within the context of exchange, devoid of any intrinsic utility. If there is an abrupt cessation of acceptance and utilization of pounds, dollars, euros, or bitcoins by all individuals, it will result in the collapse of the market bubble and engender a reduction of their worth to absolute zero. However, the occurrence of such an event is highly improbable. Even in Somalia, where governmental structures vanished two decades ago, Somali shillings remain recognized as a valid medium of exchange.

5. How is the process of cryptocurrency production carried out and what are the algorithms employed to verify its value?

The confirmation/consensus algorithm is a procedure employed for the incremental extraction of the cryptocurrency, as prearranged and unanimously approved by all network participants.

What is the essence?

To utilize the coin while facilitating its price appreciation, the subsequent circumstances must be fulfilled:

restriction in quantity;

gradual extraction;

The appreciation is always directed towards the expenditure incurred for procuring production resources, which are inherently challenging to obtain.

It showcases an innovative technology or addresses an outstanding issue thus far (such as anonymity, rapid payment processing, cost-effective transactions, robust security, absence of regulatory control).

5.1 To whom does the term 'miners' refer? What advantages are gained from finely chopping and tending to the block?

Miners refer to electronic circuit boards that are utilized for the purpose of generating new blocks within the network, specifically designed for the mining of bitcoins. Miners employ the computational resources of their computers to discover and generate fresh blocks within the blockchain, thereby populating these blocks with preferred transactions initiated by network users. This process confers a dual advantage to the miners.

Upon the discovery/creation of a new block, they receive a compensation of 12.5 bitcoins.

In the event that the volume of transactions exceeds a certain threshold, network users demonstrate readiness to remunerate the miners in order to secure priority inclusion of their payments in the succeeding block. The commission is contingent upon the quantity of transactions, the dimension of the block (currently allotted as 1 MB), and the magnitude of your transaction. It undergoes perpetual fluctuation.

In this particular scenario, it proves beneficial for the miners to expedite the process of populating the currently available block, thereby facilitating an earlier commencement of the subsequent block compared to their counterparts. The individual who successfully discovers a new block shall receive a reward of 12.5 bitcoins. Hence, miners with limited computational power aggregate into mining pools in order to enhance their likelihood of discovering blocks collectively, subsequently distributing the resulting rewards based on the proportionate resources contributed by each participant in the mining pool.

5.2 Could you please provide information on the consensus algorithms employed?

Proof of Work involves the allocation of resources such as electricity, time, and investment in specialized computer hardware for the purpose of discovering and obtaining new blocks and bitcoins. Example: Bitcoin

Issue/advantage: Considerable resources and electrical consumption are utilized; there exists a potential hazard of 51% decentralization being concentrated in the control of a single miner.

Proof of Stake is predicated on the principle that the more substantial our coin holdings within an account, the higher the probability of locating the subsequent unit. Moreover, it is essential for the wallet to remain persistently connected to the network, ensuring seamless operation, or alternatively, hosting can be leased.

Issue/advantage: Considerable amounts of resources and electricity are expended; there exists a potential risk of 51% decentralization falling under the control of a single miner.

Evidence of Significance – the algorithm bears resemblance to the Proof of Stake methodology. However, it goes beyond considering the mere presence of coins in an account, by also evaluating the duration for which the coins have been held in the wallet, as well as analyzing the extent and quantity of transactions conducted with said currency. As your number of transactions using the currency within the network increases, so does your reputation, subsequently impacting the passive mining of new coins. Example: NEM.

Problem/benefit. It enables us to mitigate decentralization by ensuring fair distribution of new coins among all engaged participants within the network, catering to genuine enthusiasts of the cryptocurrency.

Proof of Activity represents a commonly used hybrid framework that amalgamates the functionalities of both Proof of Work and Proof of Stake. Example: Dash.

Issue/advantage: We conducted a preliminary assessment by ascertaining the original value of the currency and transitioned to a more conservative algorithm.

Delegated Proof of Stake is a broad term delineating the progress of fundamental consensus protocols through the validation of shared ownership. Example: BitShares.

Proof of Burn is demonstrated by transferring coins to an address where their expenditure cannot be definitively ensured. By disposing of their coins in this manner, the user attains the entitlement to perpetual mining, wherein it is also structured as a lottery encompassing all holders of incinerated coins.

Proof of Capacity entails the implementation of the widely recognized concept of computing resources denoted in megabytes. In order to participate in the mining process, it is imperative to allocate a substantial quantum of disk space.

Evidence of Storage - akin to the preceding notion, wherein the designated storage area is utilized by all participants as a communal cloud storage resource.

Ethereum Smart Contracts

The initial purpose of developing blockchain technology was to enable its usage in conjunction with bitcoin, owing to its distinction as the pioneering cryptocurrency. However, with the advent of Ethereum, novel technology was developed to enable the creation of smart contracts. Ethereum will center its attention on facilitating peer-to-peer transactions within the realm of digital currency.

This chapter will provide insights into the creation of an Ethereum contract, irrespective of the blockchain being utilized, as the procedure remains consistent.

Additionally, you will acquire the skills to thoroughly examine your contract, ensuring that it aligns with your desired specifications prior to its implementation on the blockchain.

An illustration showcasing the implementation of a smart contract in the insurance sector.

Definitions

There are a few terms that are imperative to familiarize yourself with in order to effectively deploy your contract onto the blockchain for utilization.

Public key encryption: The public key will consist of a two-component system. The private key serves as a public key. Individuals will be required to create a virtual signature to authenticate their blockchain endeavors. It is imperative for users to create backups of their keys, as failing to do so will render them unable to access their accounts. Furthermore, external access to them will be unattainable.

The Ethereum Virtual Machine (EVM) facilitates the execution of smart contracts using the blockchain infrastructure that aligns with the specific requirements of each contract.

The decentralized application, known as Dapp, will serve as a platform for implementing smart contracts that are authored and deployed within the Ethereum marketplace. Dapp will operate either from a central location or through Ethereum nodes.

Blockchain refers to a publicly accessible decentralized ledger designed to record and store all financial transactions carried out within a cryptocurrency network.

Ethereum employs Ether as its designated digital currency. Ether is commonly denoted as ETH, with a valuation of sixty-five cents in United States currency for one unit of ETH.

Commencing the contractual agreement.

Although it is not obligatory, it is advisable to create your own Ethereum node when drafting your contract, even if you do not intend to utilize it. Upon utilizing a node, you will possess the capability to establish connections with the complete Ethereum network. This collection will encompass the Ethereum development frameworks consisting of programming languages such as Java, C, Haskell, and Python.

Currently, the solidity tool functions as a programming language and is intended to serve as the predominant programming tool. It shall serve as the Ethereum iteration of JavaScript, incorporating extensions such as .se or .sol. A compiler will also be necessary.

Please ascertain the presence of the C library in order to avail yourself of the comprehensive tools necessary for composing your contract. By downloading C , the need for solc installation can be eliminated. A viable alternative option is available in the form of a web version accessible at etherchain.org, or you may opt to utilize Cosmo. The final requirement necessitates the acquisition of web3.ja, an API application designed to facilitate the creation of dapp. After compiling a solidity contract, it will be transmitted to the network. Subsequently, the contract will be retrieved using web3.js. So, henceforth, you will be provided with the opportunity to develop web applications that will facilitate seamless interaction with your contracts.

If your intention is to utilize an existing framework, it will be necessary for you to employ the distributed application framework known as Truffle. Truffle is the preferred option for employing a foundational program that can be comprehended easily, thereby enabling a greater emphasis on the individual code. Should you choose not to utilize your personal node, an alternative option would be to utilize blockapps.net. This is an alternative application programming interface (API) that will afford you the opportunity to simulate working with a node for the purpose of testing, thus eliminating the need to directly interact with your own node.

Contracts will contain distinct provisions that will exhibit considerable variations, necessitating the inclusion of certain variables within each contractual agreement in some manner. For instance, if an occurrence ensues, its outcome shall be registered in a log, thereby establishing a consensus, albeit without impacting the conduct of the agreement. Simultaneously, there exists a mechanism capable of modifying the contractual status from affirmative to negative (and vice versa) by making necessary adjustments to the predetermined parameters prior to contract activation. The transfer will be initiated between accounts upon fulfillment of specified conditions, owing to this particular functionality.

The addresses specified in the contracts will determine the placement of your wallet and whether the contract can establish communication with your wallet through its distinct address, thereby ensuring the separation of the creator's address from that of the wallet. The subsequent parameter to consider will be the scale of the agreement; the more diminutive the agreement, the more optimal its functionality will be. Additionally, a smart contract possesses the capability to retrieve data from an oracle through the utilization of a public variable that will ultimately ascertain the necessity of consulting the data and the precise origin of such information.

Additional factors that should be taken into consideration

When drafting contracts, it is essential to thoroughly examine the information at hand to ensure comprehensive incorporation of all pertinent data, thereby facilitating compliance with the agreed-upon terms. You will be provided with a comprehensive inventory of items that will ultimately dictate the overarching framework of the file you are revising. The aforementioned data is typically stored in a 2-xn mapping sequence. N corresponds to the quantity of transactions that will be completed, accompanied by the relevant particulars associated with each individual transaction.

Whilst bearing the intended result in consideration, it becomes imperative to incorporate the definition for a pair of distinct struts. The initial document will contain details pertaining to the individual who initiated the transaction, signifying that the transaction amount will be encapsulated within this framework. The secondary support will be responsible for storing the data and any pertinent information required for accurately mapping the contract. With the aid of this framework, you can delineate the database you are handling, facilitating automatic categorization of contracts according to the pre-established template.

Now that you have completed the creation of the template, it will be necessary to establish the functions that will be periodically executed, along with the corresponding prompts required to enable the seamless fulfillment of daily tasks. The appropriate transactions will be forwarded to the proprietor of the agreement. The initial proposition entailed the incorporation of the transaction's boundaries, the allocation of funds to the contractual account, and the application of relevant stipulations.

The investor's transactions will be assigned a distinctive identification number which will be securely stored in the designated space allocated for that particular record, pertaining to the corresponding contract. The system will designate a pre-allocated area where all the outcomes of the contract will be consolidated. In the event that a specified time constraint is imposed upon the transaction, the conclusive agreement will be generated. Subsequently, this will initiate the ultimate course of action, commonly known as the termination action, to prevent the contract from being renegotiated.

At this juncture, users will have the chance to determine the course of action they wish to pursue with the allocated funds. Subsequently, these findings will be examined subsequent to the implementation of the agreement. You will be designated as an investor in the classification section of the dummy contract. You will need to undertake the necessary actions of engaging with the agreement to ensure its desired responsiveness.

Proper execution

As previously observed, utilizing Truffle as the programming process will enhance the manageability of your contract, particularly if you prefer to test your code prior to aggregating all your information. In order to expedite the writing process, Truffle will employ a Java framework to assess the scenarios within the contracts. It is important to take into consideration that the verification process for the transaction typically lasts for approximately ten seconds, provided that all contractual details are accurately documented. It is imperative that you consider the duration aspect while conducting code testing for your contractual obligations.

In order to successfully deploy your smart contract using the Truffle program, it is imperative that you possess the necessary privileges to access the console window where you are developing. This will enable you to create a new node before initiating the Truffle program. Upon executing the command, truffle will be utilized, resulting in the initiation of a spawn event within the fundamentals of the smart contract init process. The code's functionality can be evaluated by compiling it in its entirety and meticulously examining it for any errors or deployment-related issues.

What subsequently occurs" "In the subsequent sequence" "Following this, what unfolds" "What transpires in the succeeding events

After the code for the contract has been composed, it is imperative to arrange it in a manner that enables its integration into the blockchain. This can be accomplished by utilizing an online compiler designed for solidity which can be accessed through etherchain.org/solc. Once your code has been formatted, you are required to upload the contract by remitting a nominal quantity of ether in order to obtain a signature box. Inside this box, you will input your private key, thereby designating the contract as your own. Afterwards, you will be receiving the outcomes via an Application Binary Interface (ABI) along with the blockchain address where the data will be permanently stored throughout the duration of the contract.

Once all the necessary information has been gathered and verified, it is imperative to proceed with the deployment of the contract using truffle. To access a new directory, you are required to open the truffle console and utilize the init command. A novel index shall be established, which will append the contract with an extension denoted by .sol. Please proceed to access the config/app.son file in order to include the contract in the designated area assigned for it. At this point, it is advised that you proceed with restarting your program and executing the tesrpc command in order to deploy truffle at the root level. However, it is essential that your contract is recorded and stored on the blockchain.

Upon the establishment of the contract, a user interface must be developed to facilitate real-time interaction with the agreement. The dapp will be housed within a database featuring an HTML-centric user interface, establishing a direct integration with the Ethereum platform. In the event that you employ truffle, the decentralized application will integrate with a comprehensive network featuring Content Delivery Network (CDN) accessibility. The user interface (UI) of Dapp will be developed in a manner reminiscent of the design principles applied in website creation.

There will be various frameworks available to facilitate the development of your dapp, thereby simplifying your interactions. As you observed earlier, the truffle shall serve as a means at your disposal, yet it shall not exclusively restrict your utilization to it alone. In addition, you will have access to the Embark platform; however, the truffle framework will serve as the most convenient tool for developing your dapp.

By employing truffle, one will be generating a smart contract. However, it is crucial to acknowledge that there exist alternative choices available to you, enabling you to make a well-informed decision regarding the most suitable application for your needs.

Truffle is an application that will significantly automate various tasks when interacting with dapp and smart contracts.

The Embark application will facilitate the deployment of your contracts, ensuring their accessibility within the JavaScript code of your preference. Furthermore, Embark will enable comprehensive monitoring of all modifications made to your contract. In the event of such an occurrence, Embark will proceed to automatically reassign your contract and deploy DApps as necessary.

Dapp creation

Once the dapp has been created, it is advisable to utilize truffle as it will automatically compile the user interface once it has been established. In order for the truffle director to compile the contact information upon the next execution, it is imperative that it be appropriately labeled as an app. In addition, it will gather any recent modifications into the build directory, making them readily accessible within the truffle application in critical situations.

Before commencing, it is necessary to designate the directory as an application, thereby enabling it to locate the background images and JavaScript code associated with the stylesheets and indexes. Depending on your requirements, you will have the opportunity to incorporate the code directly into the existing file, enabling you to acquire the front-end user interface option and swiftly deploy your contract. Upon opening the app.js file, you will come across a dedicated section that will deliver a salutation from truffle within the developer console. Upon accessing this console, a compilation of currently active commands will be displayed.

In considering directives, it is necessary to develop a function that can be invoked upon each instance of page rendering. In order to accomplish this, it is necessary to include a window through the utilization of the code window.onload within the app.js file. If executed accurately, a collection of account particulars shall be displayed on the console browser. Ultimately, you will employ an examination. Modify the Conference.js function to ensure that the generated output conforms to your desired specifications. The desired result should be the remaining amount, and this remaining amount will experience an increment after the situation is postponed.

Once the creation of app.js and index.html is completed to align with your requirements, you will proceed to validate the outcomes by employing either your own node or an exemplar node, which will promptly generate real-time outputs. Please be advised that the outcomes will not be expeditiously prepared. It is advisable to utilize the provided code in order to ensure its proper functionality.

Please execute the 'geth' command with the following options: enable RPC with the IP address "0.0.0.0", allow any domain to access the RPC API, enable mining, unlock accounts 0 and 1, set verbosity level to 5, limit the number of peers to 0, allocate 4 threads to mining, assign a network ID of '12345', and use the 'testgenesis.json' file as the genesis block.

Two additional accounts will be created, designated as zero and one. It is imperative to acknowledge that it is necessary to possess both accounts in order to generate separate passwords for each report. Consequently, this will facilitate the creation of a json test-genesis file, which will be located under the "alloc" section on the account designated for ether expenses. Recently, it has become necessary for you to incorporate the outcomes into your truffle application. This will enable you to recompile the contract and subsequently redeploy the results once again.

There exists an alternative that enables you to generate a user interface for utilization with any decentralized application (dapp) developed by the entity known as silent cicero. This application can be accessed at the website dapp-builder.metor.com. This tool will be utilized to generate HTML code that can subsequently be customized for your contracts written in solidity, web3.js, or jQuery. It may not proceed with the desired level of efficiency, however, if one harbors concerns regarding their own proficiency in independently navigating the procedure. The subsequent user interface (UI) will employ identical procedures as those previously presented. In the event that it does not, an alternative variant is typically available, which will likely facilitate your search for a resolution to your predicament.

At this juncture, the contractual agreement will be drafted, yet your tasks will not be completed at present. It is imperative that you conduct an analysis of the agreement. Upon careful examination, you can verify that the agreement has been composed accurately and does not require any further adjustments.

Upon examination of the variables situated at the commencement of your contract, they shall present themselves in the following manner:

"Extend salutations to the organizer of the public event;
The registrants' payments are publicly recorded in the mapping structure under the address as the key and the corresponding uint value.
Uint public nonresistant;
The public quota of unit.

Concerning the address, given its significance as the foremost element in your contract, it shall pertain to your wallet address. The address will be determined upon invocation of the conference() constructor. However, it is typically customary for the contract to designate the party as the owner.

Upon examination, it will become evident that the aforementioned will pertain to the data type known as unsigned integer. There must be available capacity on the blockchain; hence, it is necessary to strive for minimal data size.

In the public scope, it is expected that you define a variable accessible externally to the contract. When utilizing the private modifier, it shall be invoked as per the stipulations of the agreement. However, it is crucial to verify that the variable from web3.js is publicly accessible if you intend to make use of it through a function call.

Regarding the utilization of Solidity, it is important to note that there will be dissimilar degrees of assistance provided for arrays and mappings, such as those involving the mapping structure (address => uint). Additionally, the address is going to be recorded once registrants have made their payment. These mappings will occupy a reduced amount of space. Hence, the delineation will be employed for the purpose of preserving a record of the registrant who has made the payment, ensuring that their financial resources remain accessible in the future.

Additional information regarding addresses: This particular node pertaining to the client will retain pertinent details regarding your account. Upon commencement of your examination, a set of ten available addresses shall be provided.

The initial account will be designated as zero, and it will serve as the default option for any transaction in instances where the state has not been explicitly indicated beforehand.

Organizer address vs. Designated address: Once the contract is commissioned, it will be assigned a distinct designated address that differs from the address of the organizer. This address will be accessible via your solidity contract. It will be utilized in the refund ticket feature specified in the contract, where the address is assigned as this;

When it comes to Solidity, the act of self-destruction in the smart contract is considered beneficial: in the event of any funds being transferred to your contract, they will be securely retained by the agreement itself. By utilizing the destroy function, the resources will be effectively relinquished to the rightful proprietor of the transaction. If this measure is not implemented, the funds would become immobilized, resulting in their inaccessibility. Therefore, it is crucial that you incorporate a contingency plan for the event of the termination of your contract, ensuring that you are able to recuperate the funds in such unfortunate circumstances.

Nevertheless, in the event that you emulate a separate entity within the contractual agreement, you will be provided with the choice to employ an alternative address that diverges from the aforementioned accounts array. Consequently, in order to acquire a ticket, it will be necessary for you to procure it using this particular function.

Certain function invocations can be regarded as transactions. Such invocations have the capability to modify the state of the contract and include a designated sender as well as a value encapsulated within the curly braces. The funds will subsequently be conveyed to the address of the wallet. Therefore, using solidity grants you the capability to access values by means of the msg. The functions for the solidity are stored by the sender and Ms. Value.

Occasions: Participation in events will be discretionary as you proceed with the contractual drafting process. Within the agreement, the deposits will be scheduled for transmission and recorded by the virtual machine. However, their lack of action should not be a cause for concern. Instead, consider this opportunity as a valuable exercise in honing your ability to meticulously maintain records of all past transactions.

Investing in Cryptocurrencies
Prior to moving forward, it is imperative to acknowledge that cryptocurrencies exhibit notable levels of volatility, limited liquidity, and an absence of comprehensive regulatory frameworks. These factors collectively contribute to a highly precarious investment environment in relation to cryptocurrencies. It is frequently recommended that individuals should allocate funds for investment purposes that they are prepared to relinquish without significant financial repercussions. When approached with prudence, investing in cryptocurrency has the potential to yield considerable profits.

Strategies for Investing in Cryptocurrencies.
If you have an interest in allocating funds towards cryptocurrencies, there

exists a wide array of possibilities for you to consider. These include:

• Engaging in the practice of cryptocurrency mining as a means of investment

• Investing in and retaining virtual currencies • Purchasing and maintaining crypto assets • Acquiring and retaining digital currencies

• Acquiring shares of a stock that possesses a digital currency.

• Conducting transactions involving digital currencies

Investing in and retaining digital currencies

An approach to venture into cryptocurrencies includes acquiring and retaining a particular cryptocurrency with the expectation of its value appreciating in the long run. Digital currencies can be acquired by utilizing platforms such as Coinbase, Binance, KuCoin, and similar services. If you plan on buying and holding digital currencies, then it is important that you learn to time right.

Acquire a cryptocurrency solely if you believe that its value will persistently increase. If the existing data indicate a potential decrease in the value of a specific currency, it would be prudent to exercise patience until the prices commence their upward trend. Foremost, it is strongly recommended that you diligently conduct comprehensive research prior to embarking on any investment venture.

Trading Cryptocurrencies
The act of engaging in cryptocurrency trading deviates from the practice of simply acquiring and retaining digital currencies, as trading involves not retaining a cryptocurrency with the expectation of its value rising. On the contrary, you proactively endeavor to procure digital currencies at a reduced

cost and subsequently vend them at an elevated price within a brief timeframe. This type of investment necessitates a significant amount of time, along with the need for patience, a comprehensive understanding of the cryptocurrency sphere and market. It is strongly recommended that you dedicate significant effort to your studies, as doing so will enhance your ability to effectively navigate the volatile landscape.

Investing in a Security that Holds a Digital Currency

This investment opportunity offers the ability to securely store cryptocurrencies within a tax-advantaged investment account, with the added benefit of designating beneficiaries. As an illustration, the Grayscale Bitcoin Investment Trust (GBTC) can be cited, which is a trust intentionally structured to offer investors exposure to bitcoin within a conventional security. GBTC facilitates the trading of bitcoin within the equity market for investors. The total number of bitcoins held by GBTC amounts to approximately 175,000. GBTC is structured in a manner that aligns with the SPDR Gold Shares ETF, rendering it a publicly traded investment vehicle focused on bitcoin.

Every individual unit of GBTC symbolizes a fraction of one bitcoin, specifically one-tenth. The trust operated by Grayscale Investments is eligible to be held in various types of accounts, such as IRA, 401(k), Roth IRA, as well as brokerage and investment accounts. Investors, whether accredited or non-accredited, have the opportunity to procure GBTC on the OTCQX platform through their brokerage and investment accounts, such as IRA and Roth IRA. This means that the shares can be freely traded. Accredited individuals have the opportunity to directly purchase shares from the issuer. Nevertheless, despite the fact that these shares are subject to restrictions on resale and transfer.

GBTC presents a viable opportunity for investors seeking to augment their portfolio diversification by utilizing bitcoin. The escalating valuation of bitcoin in recent times can be attributed to the growing interest exhibited by individuals with substantial financial resources, commonly referred to as ultra-high-net-worth individuals. This phenomenon persists, despite the current value of bitcoin fluctuating around $6,500 at the time this statement is being made.

Trading Cryptocurrencies on Exchange Platforms: Techniques and Strategies
It is highly probable that you are interested in engaging in bitcoin cryptocurrency trading, yet find yourself uncertain about the ideal point of initiation. In the eventuality of this being the case, an initial requirement for engaging in digital currency trading is to locate a reputable cryptocurrency exchange platform through which one can conveniently acquire and vend the specific token of interest.

A cryptocurrency exchange platform is an internet-based platform that facilitates the acquisition, divestment, or transference of cryptocurrencies in exchange for other cryptoassets or conventional currencies such as the US dollar or Euro.

Numerous platforms are at your disposal to fulfill this objective; hence, we have undertaken thorough research to identify the cryptocurrency exchange that is most suitable for your trading requirements. They include:

1. Changelly is a cryptocurrency exchange platform.

Changelly is a cryptocurrency platform that endeavors to facilitate convenient access to cryptocurrencies for crypto enthusiasts. The ownership of the exchange rests with MinerGate, the mining pool.

Changelly offers a streamlined user experience, enabling potential clients to seamlessly access the platform by simply logging in using their email ID. This negates the need for any extensive verification or registration procedures, allowing users to initiate exchanges promptly.

The platform presently accommodates a diverse range of more than 35 cryptocurrencies, alongside facilitating fiat pairs such as USD/EUR. One advantageous aspect of this transaction is its inherent trustworthiness and simplicity. When clients express their desire to engage in cryptocurrency exchanges, the advanced algorithms of Changelly facilitate connections with established and vibrant cryptocurrency exchanges, ultimately enabling them to access the most favorable and up-to-date rates.

The process of exchanging one cryptocurrency for another on the platform typically requires a duration of 5 to 30 minutes. Changelly imposes a commission rate of 0.5 percent on every transaction. In addition to the commission, users are also responsible for covering the miner's fee, which is subtracted directly from their cryptocurrency balance.

Traders have the ability to purchase cryptocurrency utilizing VISA and MasterCard, encompassing both credit and debit card options. Furthermore, they have the option to purchase cryptocurrencies using any cryptocurrency or wallet that is supported by Changelly.

2. The trading platform known as Bitfinex
Bitfinex is widely recognized and esteemed as one of the largest cryptocurrency exchanges in operation. The platform established in Hong Kong has been operating since the year 2014. Customers have the ability to conduct 13 different cryptocurrency trades in exchange for either USD or BTC. The aforementioned cryptocurrencies consist of Bitcoin, Bitcoin cash, Litecoin, Ethereum, Zcash, OmiseGO, Dash,

Monero, Ethereum Classic, EOS, IOTA, Ripple, and Santiment.

Bitfinex provides the opportunity to engage in trading activities with USD, subject to a wire fee of maximum $20. Furthermore, there will be a requisite trade fee ranging from 0.1% to 0.8%.

Bitfinex provides a range of advanced trading tools, including but not limited to limit orders, trailing stop, stop orders, TWAP, fill or kill, alongside various market charts. Prior to your account being fully operational, it is necessary that a minimum deposit of 10000 USD or its equivalent in cryptocurrencies is made.

3. HitBTC is a cryptocurrency exchange platform.

Established in 2013, HitBTC is a cryptocurrency exchange platform headquartered in Hong Kong. The system boasts of its status as the "foremost state-of-the-art digital currency exchange." HitBTC provides a rebate system for participants who create liquidity in the market, along with a sophisticated matching algorithm.

Users are strictly prohibited from engaging in trading activities involving fiat currency, and are unable to establish a connection between their platform account and a bank account. Hence, in order to purchase bitcoins, it will be necessary for them to utilize a credit card.

4. Coinbase is the entity in question.

Coinbase serves as a multifunctional platform, encompassing both wallet and exchange capabilities. Furthermore, they provide an assortment of resources and instruments for traders. The establishment of the company in 2012 precipitated its emergence as a leading and highly sought-after cryptocurrency platform.

Cryptocurrency enthusiasts have the ability to engage in the purchase, sale, storage, and exchange of digital currencies through the Coinbase platform. Coinbase has the distinction of being the pioneering cryptocurrency to surpass a valuation of $1 billion. The primary appeal for the majority of users lies in the platform's remarkable ease of use, rendering it the preferred choice for novice individuals. It is unsurprising that it manages a portfolio of more than 20 million accounts.

5. CEX.io is a reputable and established online platform.
CEX.IO provides substantial market liquidity, robust security measures, and the ability to engage in cross-platform trading. It ensures a nearly perfect uptime rate, etc. The exchange has its headquarters in London, United Kingdom.

6. LocalBitcoins, a platform facilitating peer-to-peer cryptocurrency transactions,
LocalBitcoins is a decentralized cryptocurrency exchange platform facilitating peer-to-peer (P2P) transactions, enabling users to engage in individualized trading with one another.

LocalBitcoins also offers a dispute resolution system and ratings mechanisms for traders, alongside additional features. Users have the ability to expeditiously publish a rapid purchase or rapid sale advertisement on the platform.

LocalBitcoins places paramount importance on safeguarding the privacy of its users. In order to bolster privacy, it provides users with the option to procure bitcoin in a face-to-face transaction, thereby avoiding any association with their personal information on an exchange.

7. "Cryptopia as an alternative option.

Cryptopia is a New Zealand-based platform that facilitates the exchange of cryptocurrencies. It provides an extensive selection of digital currencies, encompassing Bitcoin, Litecoin, and Tether trading pairs. Cryptopia offers its services globally and imposes a trading fee of 0.2 percent.

Furthermore, Cryptopia provides a platform wherein individuals are able to utilize cryptocurrency for the purpose of purchasing a wide range of items.

8. Bitpanda is the formal alternative.

Bitpanda is a cryptocurrency exchange platform situated in Vienna, Austria, that operates with complete automation. Its inherent automation allows for swift processing and validation of payments. Bitpanda facilitates the trading of a maximum of eight cryptocurrencies within its platform, while also providing traditional currency wallets for major currencies such as the euro, US dollar, and GB Pound, among others. The cryptocurrencies that are endorsed encompass BTC, ETH, LTC, DASH, BCH, XRP, MIOTA, KMD.

Bitpanda provides an additional benefit by offering support for a diverse range of payment methods, with the aim of facilitating the seamless buying and selling of cryptocurrencies for crypto users based in Europe. As a result, the platform offers various payment alternatives including Visa and Mastercard credit cards, SOFORT transfer, EPS, Neteller, Online Bank Transfer, Giropay, Skrill, SEPA, and the exclusive feature of Bitpanda to go, which exclusively facilitates transactions denominated in Euro. The purchasing fee for the cryptocurrency is 1.49%, whereas the selling fee is 1.29%.

9. Coinmama is a authorized digital currency exchange platform.

Coinmama is a cryptocurrency exchange platform that has established a presence in the market since 2013. The objective of this exchange is to ensure secure and efficient accessibility to digital currencies such as Bitcoin and Ethereum.

Coinmama is a centralized platform that is under the ownership of NBV International, a company registered in Slovakia and conducts its operations from Israel. It prides itself on having an extensive user community exceeding one million individuals, partially attributed to its comprehensive global assistance.

Coinmama provides a rapid, robust, and reliable method for purchasing cryptocurrencies such as Bitcoin, Ethereum, Litecoin, Bitcoin Cash, etc. via credit cards. Coinmama exclusively offers a purchasing service. Consequently, the platform solely facilitates the purchase of cryptocurrencies.

Furthermore, Coinmama does not offer an integrated wallet for the range of cryptocurrencies it supports. In order to acquire cryptocurrencies, it is imperative that you possess a compatible wallet that supports the specific cryptocurrency you intend to purchase. Coinmama implements this practice to promote the adoption of secure wallets among investors prior to their cryptocurrency purchases.

10. Paxful is an online platform.

Paxful was established in 2015. The platform provides a peer-to-peer marketplace wherein individuals can post their trade offers as buyers or sellers, with the platform itself serving solely as an intermediary between the relevant parties.

The platform enables users to engage in purchasing and selling Bitcoin by availing themselves of a multitude of payment options, encompassing credit/debit card, PayPal, bank transfer, Skrill, Neteller, and various gift cards (such as iTunes, Amazon, Steam, etc.).

Paxful does not impose any direct charges on buyers wishing to acquire bitcoin. Conversely, sellers have the prerogative to levy buyers with arbitrary sums. As a result, the percentage levied may differ significantly based on the method of payment utilized.

Nonetheless, Paxful imposes a 1 percent fee on sellers. Furthermore, the seller incurs a 'mining fee' during the transmission of bitcoin. Paxful promotes a culture of transparency within its platform. Consequently, participants engaged in trading transactions have the opportunity to post reviews on the profile of the counterparty with whom they conducted Bitcoin trades. Feedback is publicly showcased in an effort to foster transparency, foster integrity, and provide individuals with the opportunity to assess the reliability of a person prior to engaging in any transaction with them.